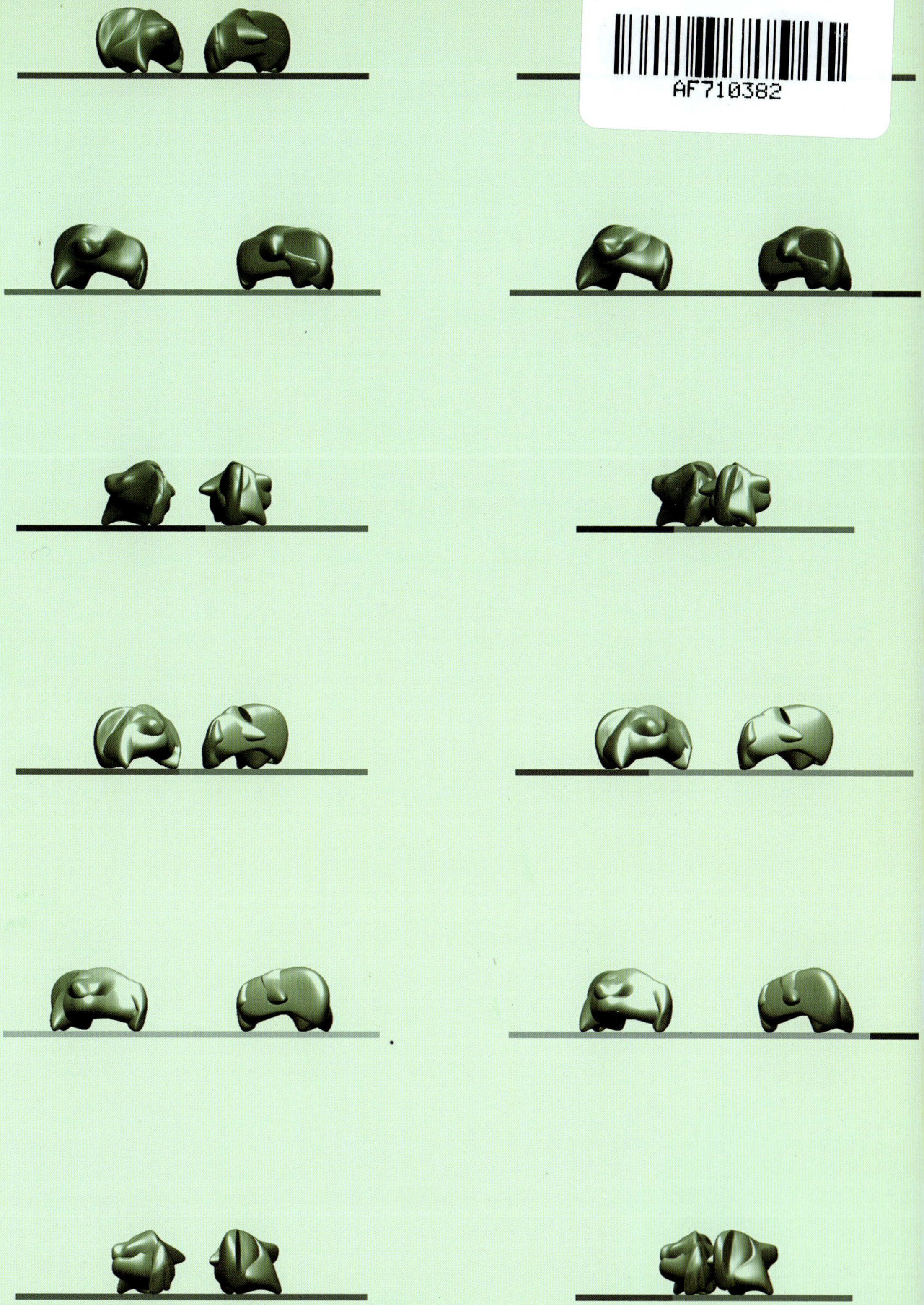

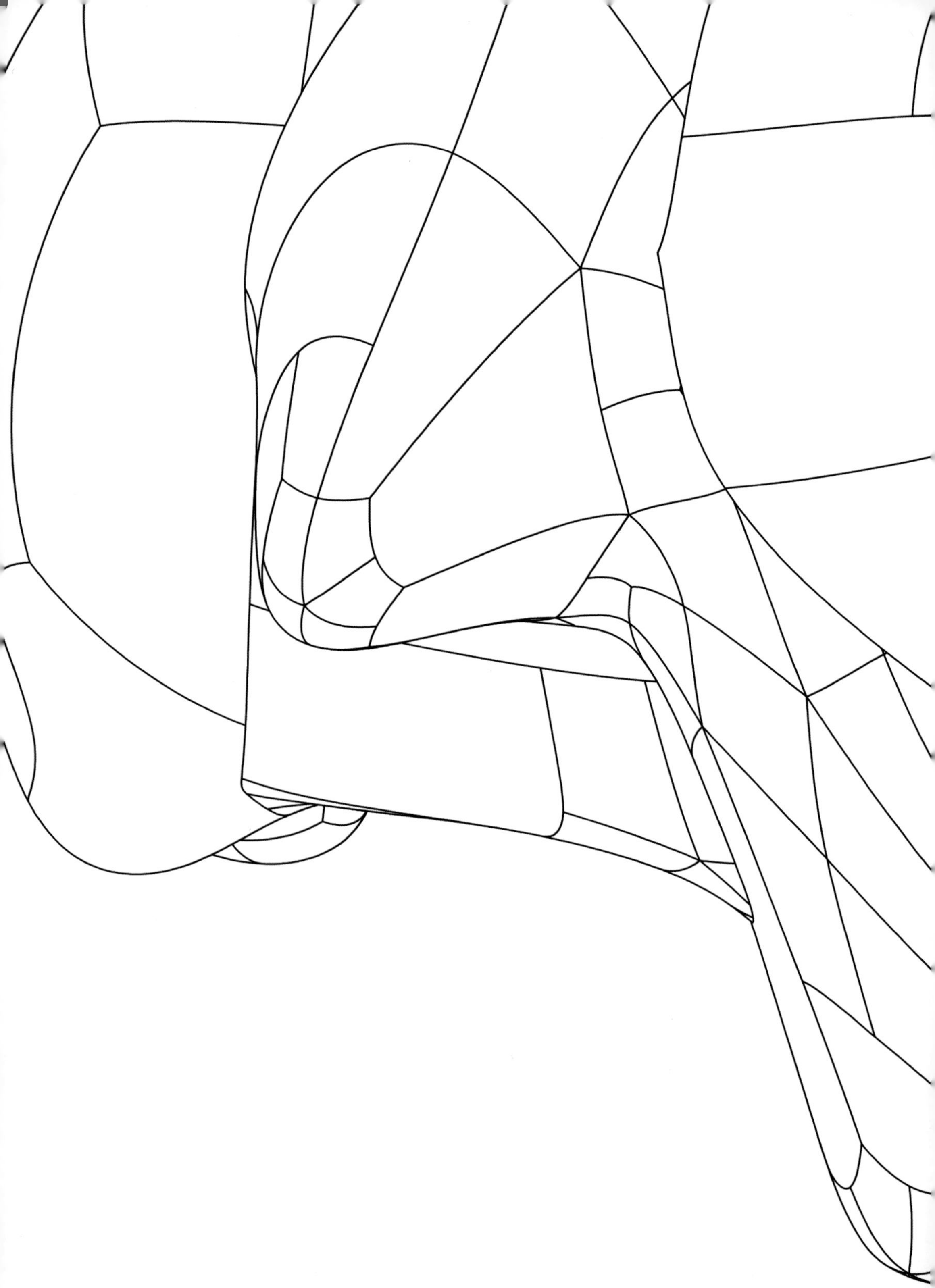

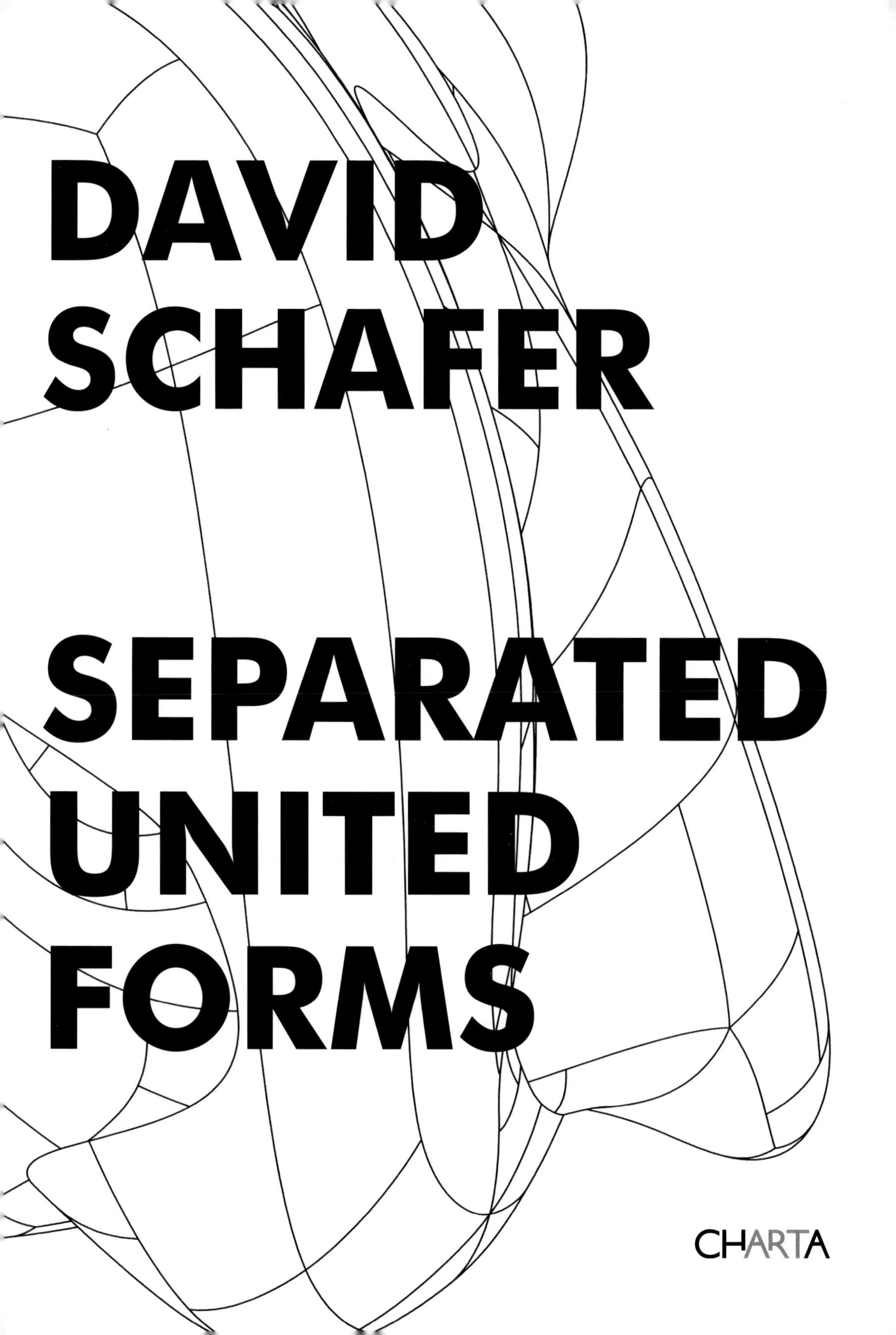

DAVID SCHAFER

SEPARATED UNITED FORMS

CHARTA

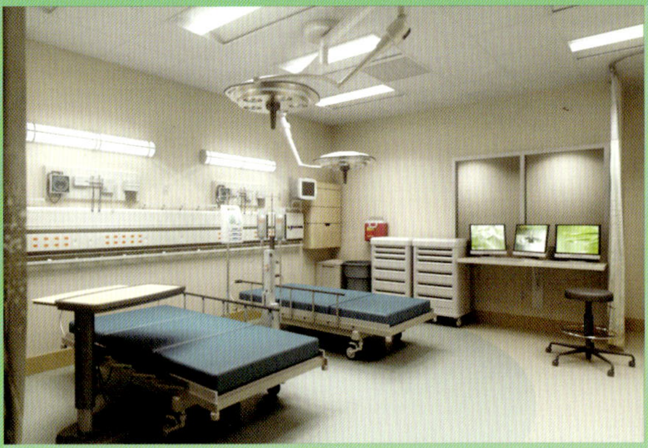

Contents

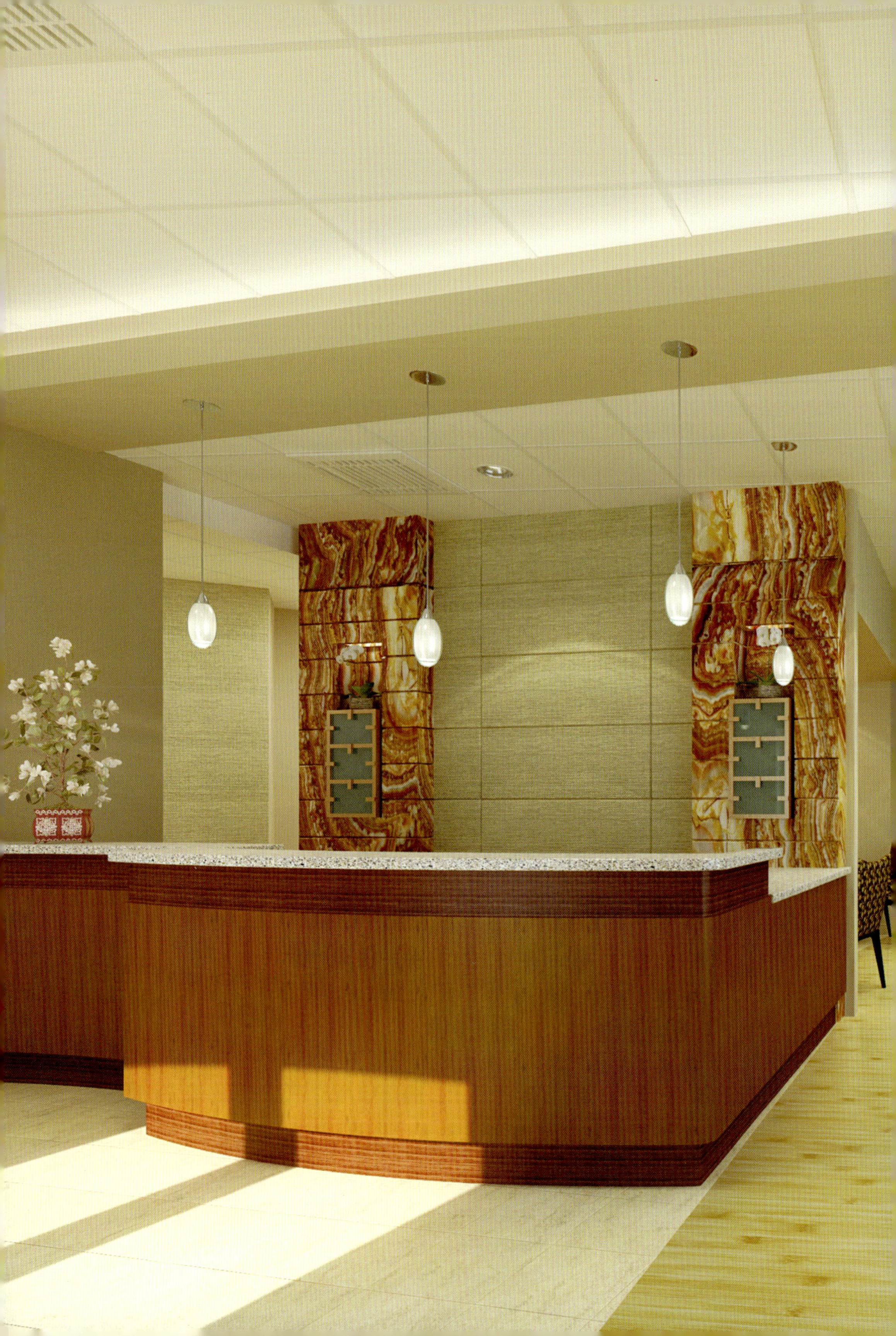

WHERE DOES IT HURT?

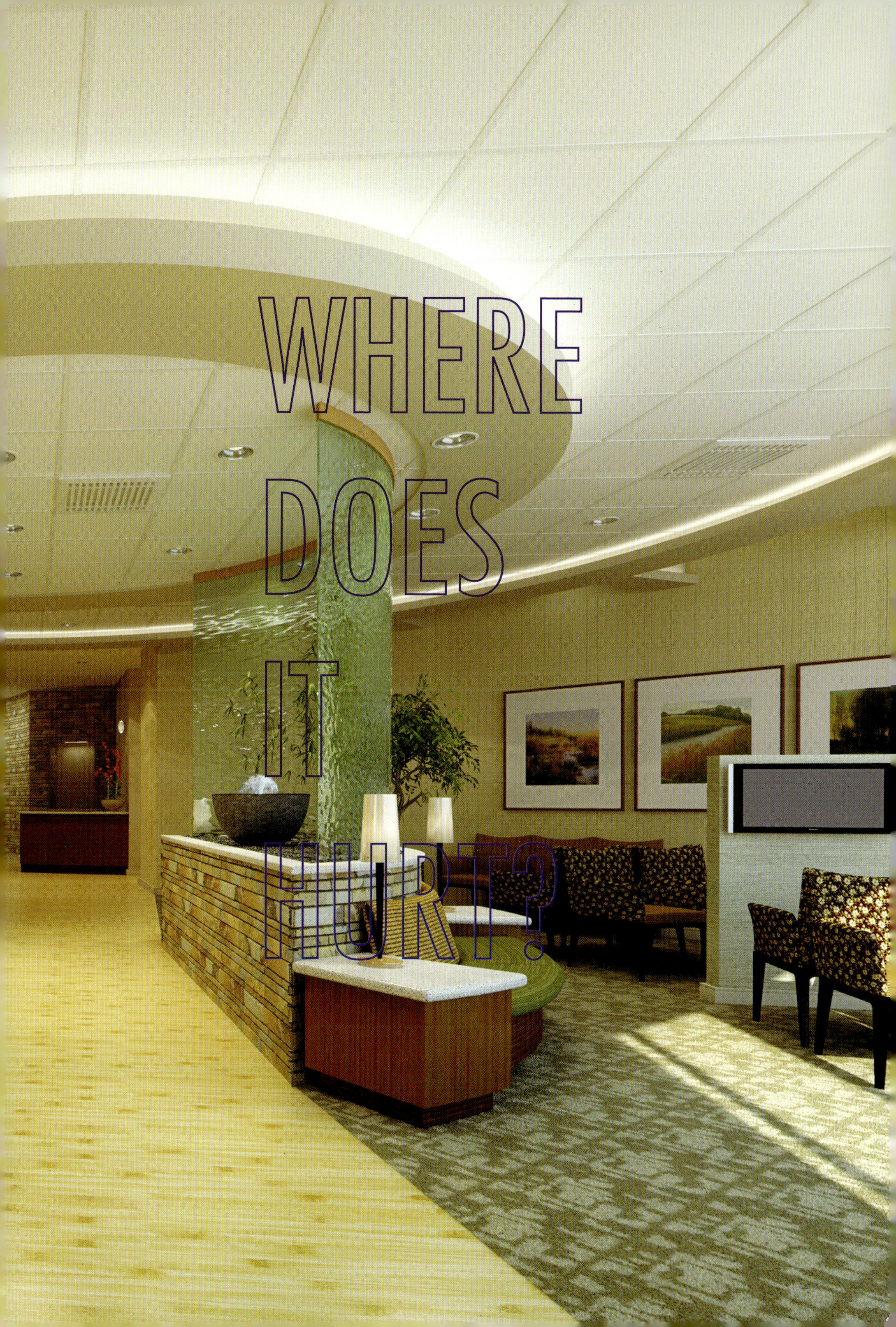

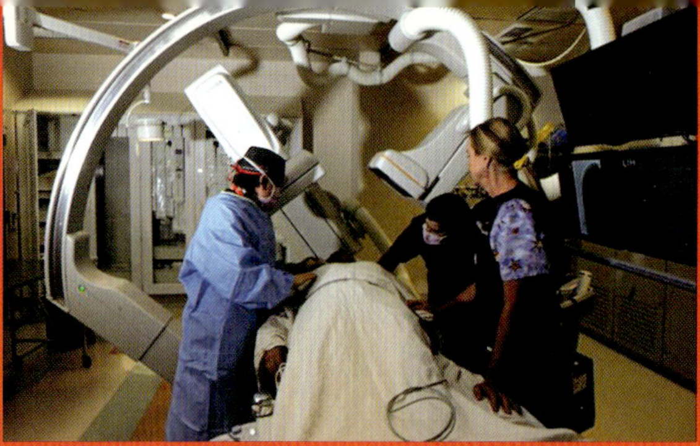

Where Does it Hurt?

David Schafer

The idea of the hospital immediately conjures up thoughts of the human body: its beauty, its flaws, and its diseases. Birth, growth, life, and death—a basic cyclical structure exists—and the spiritual and material needs for medical and social space to coincide have evolved. The New Huntington Pavilion in Pasadena represents an advanced fusion of medical analysis with the spectacle of comfort. By restaging the social body as a site-specific public sculpture, the patients and staff of the Huntington Hospital are enticed to exit the confinement of the clinical space, to become observers themselves of the colonized body.[1] From the observed to the observer, the unveiling of the abstracted forms is redistributed on stage for all to gaze upon: bodies and eyes meet.

Within the walls of the hospital, the clinical gaze and the spatialization of the pathological facilitate a means to sustain the living organism on the cellular and molecular levels. According to the Vitalist doctrine of the early twentieth century, the life in living organisms is caused and sustained by a vital force that is distinct from all physical and chemical forces, and that life is, in part, self-determining and self-evolving. The Vital Life Force and the philosophy of Vitalism were the basis for a new language of abstraction in art at that time.[2] Even today, the vigor, suppleness, and fluidity of the abject human body, as well as the complex associations of the animate form, are understood to live within an array of organic universalities. The site of the hospital is where

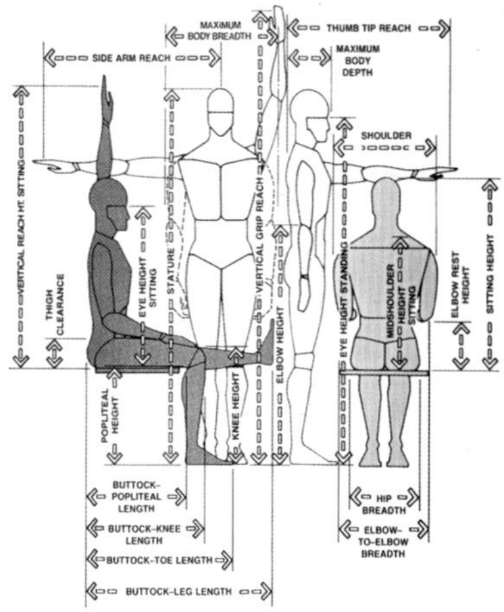

Anthropometry Chart

the Vital but disorganized and diseased body is reorganized by the multiple gazes of doctors and medical professionals within the confines of the clinic.

The Vital sculptural form evokes the life force; it recalls not human representation, but inert matter imagined as impregnated with life. In the early to mid-twentieth century, artists including Henry Moore, Barbara Hepworth, Jean Arp, among others associated with surrealism, developed a new language of organic abstraction that embraced the idea of the Vital Life Force.[3] This biomorphic aesthetic eventually permeated the realm of popular culture with products, architecture, automobiles, furniture, and graphic design, all expressing the embryonic fluidity and optimism for the future that was reflective of Vitalist doctrine. The Norton Simon Museum in Pasadena has acquired a vast collection of Henry Moore sculptures. Moore was perhaps one of the most recognizable artists to embrace the metaphor of the Vital Life Force in his work. His *Reclining Form* (1966), a small white marble sculpture in the Norton Simon collection, is a quiet and reductive form that evokes a sensuous and abstracted body. The sculpture, symptomatic of modernism, is based on the reclining female form, which was true of most of Moore's work; his interpretive response to the figure enacted the abstracted body.

Separated United Forms (2009) is a public sculpture that takes its form from Moore's *Reclining Form*, but further abstracts it through a process of sampling and remixing. The site

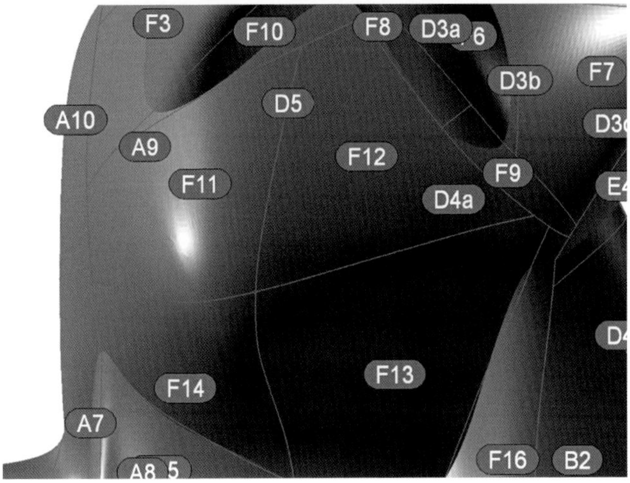

for the sculpture is embedded within the grounds of the new pavilion of the Huntington Hospital, which is both a privately funded symbolic structure and a public space, as well as a site of political, social, and cultural engagement.

In 2005, Art Center College of Design—also located in Pasadena and known for embracing new technologies—had acquired a hand-held three-dimensional body scanner to be used by the Design, Transportation, and Fine Art Departments. The scanner is identical to the body imaging systems used within the medical industry and is the technical armature of the medical gaze.[4] Access to this state-of-the-art equipment facilitated the opportunity to digitally capture the Moore sculpture with a minimum of subjective interpretation.

The variety of processes that were utilized for the capture—including sampling and remixing, as well as the casting and fabrication for *Separated United Forms*—play a significant role in the conceptual aspects of this project. Therefore it is important to describe and discuss these processes as ideas in regards to the sculpture itself, as well as its site and placement. The digital imaging and development, the selection of the bronze, the mold manufacturing, and the casting itself all participate in how the piece signifies at the site of the hospital and in relation to its site within the community of Pasadena.

The process of scanning the Moore sculpture involved extensive communication between the institutions involved: Art Center College of Design, The Norton Simon Museum, and the

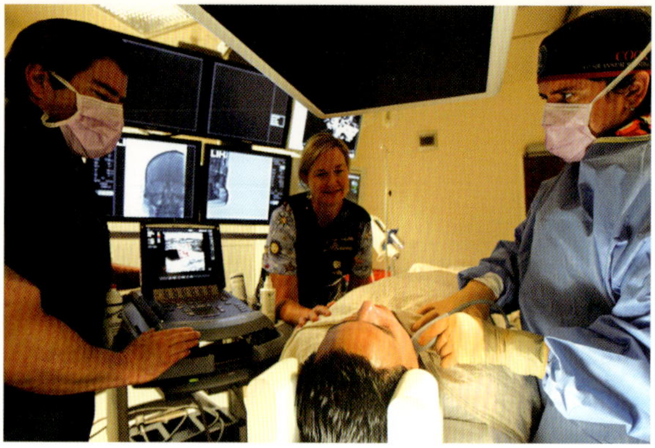

Archive photo, Huntington Hospital

Huntington Hospital. The triangulation of institutional communication and collaboration between a school, a museum, and a hospital functions as a matrix of site specificity, beyond the site of the body or the hospital itself.[5] Multiple levels of intra-institutional communication took place in order to stage the imaging process of the Moore sculpture. The Norton Simon vault acted as a theater of observation, in which the scanning mimicked a medical procedure, witnessed by curators and security guards. Technicians from Art Center and latex-gloved museum assistants manipulated the inert object as the scanner was aimed at it. The scanner's intense red rays engulfed the marble sculpture, and the scan data was quickly retrieved. As if from a science fiction scene, the Life Force reanimation process began, and the object transformed from object to data, from analogue to digital.[6]

Mimicking meiotic cell division, the two ends of *Reclining Form* were disembodied and, through a series of rotations, reflections, and shifts, were superimposed onto each other.[7] The forms were then doubled, incorporating additional shifts, shears, and adjustments, generating a tension of similarities and differences between them. This surgical action allowed *Reclining Form* to replicate—through a fission-like maneuver—into two unique forms. The doubling of the biomorphic sampled forms reflects the organization of the living body, such as the symmetry of vital organs, limbs, and facial features. Through

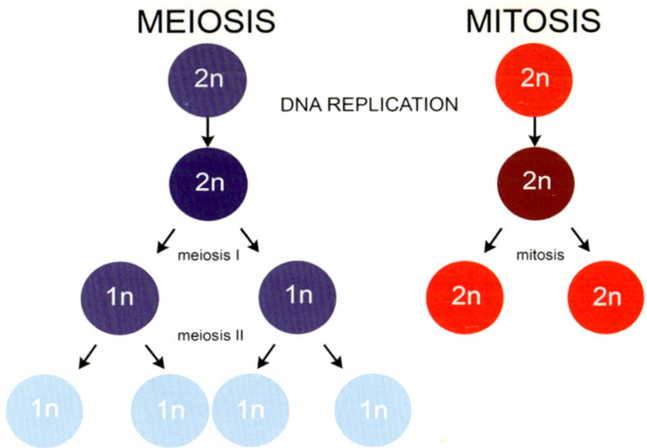

a series of CNC- [computer numerical control] programmed milling paths, the model for *Separated United Forms* emerged as a pre-visualization of the eminent larger object. The physical model could be studied, surfaced, and colorized, allowing for a more precise consideration of its potential location and placement within the context of the hospital. The sectioning and casting process for *Separated United Forms* utilized the most advanced systems available for visualization and CNC programs at the Walla Walla foundry in Walla Walla, Washington. These files generated the dozens of molds necessary for the casting process. Bypassing the full-scale pattern stage that is typically necessary in the production of a sculpture this scale, the foundry was capable of going directly from the digital files to the mold sections themselves.[8] The full-scale sculpture did not physically exist until the final process of bronze casting and fabrication was completed. The alchemy of the lost wax procedure was augmented by the collaboration and synthesis of the digital imaging and work-flow processes.[9]

When the CNC milling of the molds was completed, the remaining processes of casting, fabrication, and finishing followed a traditional industrial procedure that has not evolved much since the era of Henry Moore. The cast bronze sections were carefully fitted together and welded. *Separated United Forms* was assembled and its welded seams ground until they disappeared, not unlike the stitches and grafts in medical pro-

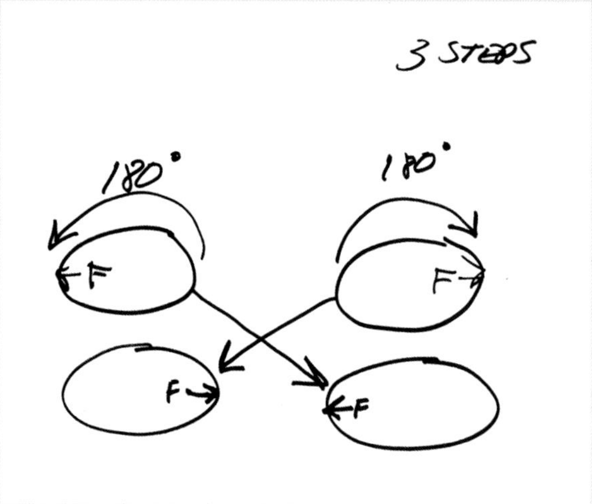

Concept Diagram

cedures. When installed, the dark patina of *Separated United Forms* would absorb the light and soften the forms, drawing attention to the fluidity and its animate sculptural characteristics.

The location for *Separated United Forms* is an outdoor, publicly accessible site that is embedded within the Huntington Hospital grounds. It is visibly available to the street and sidewalk traffic, along with viewing access from the interior buildings surrounding the site. Accommodating the hospital visitors, doctors, staff, patients, and pedestrians, the site is also visible from the street and neighboring buildings. The spatiality of the project itself represents the modernist ideal, as an idea of democratic public space.[10] The landscaping surrounding the site provides shade and places to sit. The site evokes a park-like atmosphere, heightening the possibility for viewer observation and contemplation. The site, open at the front and side, performs as a picture window and frames the public view. The landscape program considers the visibility of the sculpture as well as of the viewers observing the sculpture from the street. Confounding representation, the sculptures require the observational gaze of the viewers, while inside the hospital, it is the viewers who are gazed upon.

Separated United Forms is positioned on an expansive concrete grid platform, creating an observation deck for its viewers. The ground plane grid sits in contrast to the vector-based biomorphic forms resting upon it. The platform isolates

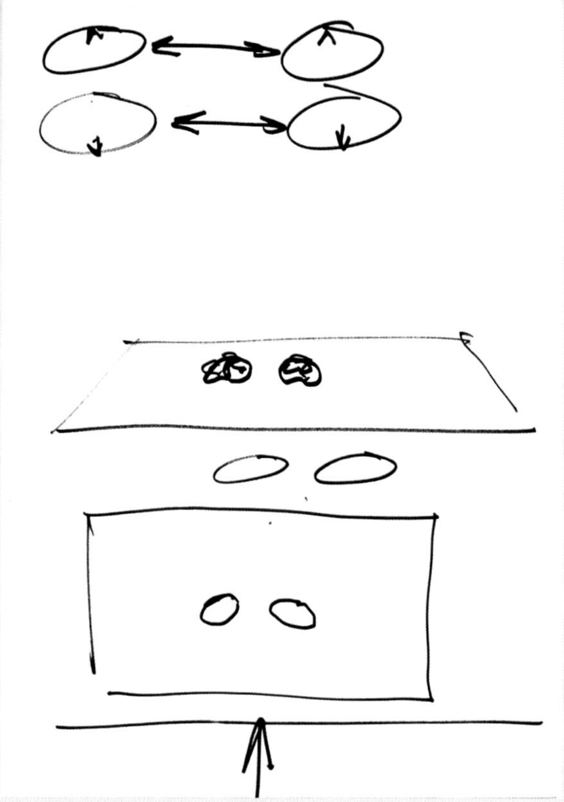

the separated forms on a geometric surface, resembling an examining situation of hybrid bodies for the observation of the viewing public. Embedded into the concrete slab and designed for optimum enhancement are eight in-ground lights positioned around the two forms. The in-grounds illuminate from below, providing a contrasting visual and spatial experience to ordinary daylight. Viewing the sculptures at night evokes a dark theatricality, framed by the illuminated parking garage behind them. The sculptures function as surrogates for the private and social body and will continue to be reorganized by the multiple gazes emanating from the viewing pedestrians.

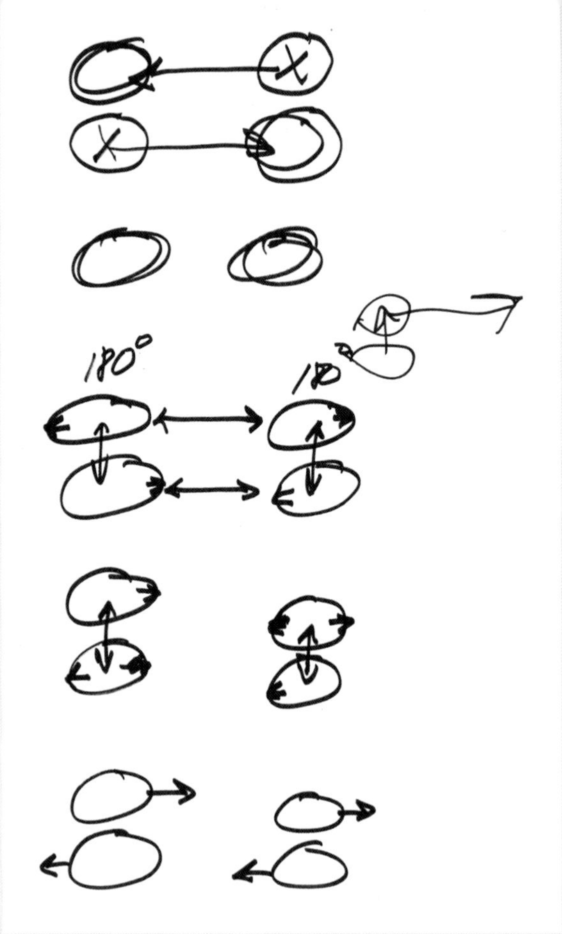

Notes:

[1] This is a reference to the *Separated United Forms* (2009) sculptures as a colonized-re-colonized body that the viewers are invited to observe. The viewers themselves are colonized by the intersecting gazes within the clinical space of the hospital, and their tangible bodies are consumed by the domination of the gaze. For discussion of the medicalization of society, see Michel Foucault, *The Birth of the Clinic: An Archaeology of Medical Perception*, trans. A. M. Sheridan Smith (New York: Pantheon Books, 1973).

[2] Vitalism, based on nonphysical substance and states of life, is a metaphysical doctrine concerned with the irreducible effects and manifestations of living things. Henry Moore's Vitalism, or Vital Life Force, is in no way scientifically analytical; it is the Vitalism of the naturalist and

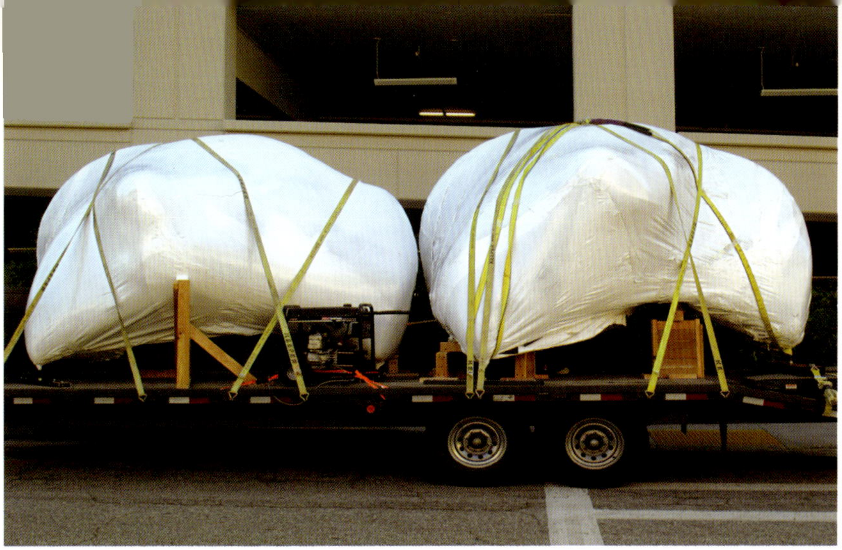

SUF arriving at site

the sensitive craftsman. Besides the sculpture itself, the most obvious example of this lies in Moore's writings. See Jack Burnham, *Beyond Modern Sculpture: The Effects of Science and Technology on the Sculpture of This Century* (New York: George Braziller, Inc., 1968).

[3] The Vitalist aesthetic, a new formal invention that influenced Arp, Hepworth, and Moore, among others, included similar traits of fabrication and execution. This included no outward hints or gouged surfaces or finger marks that would indicate any external forming agent. All is made and rearranged from the inside, the growth center of the piece. As in truth to material, each piece has its own qualities, which are imbued with psychic energy. See Burnham, *Beyond Modern Sculpture*.

[4] The scanning device that was used on the *Reclining Form* is a Creaform handheld imaging scanner supplied by Art Center College of Design. The scanner is the first mobile device able to digitize the body in real time. When used in hospitals, doctors can upload the data into a three-dimensional computer-aided design program to custom design orthopedic braces and bone implants or to print out a three-dimensional model. The scanner was used to scan the Henry Moore sculpture, which is an abstraction of a human figure.

[5] The site is a matrix or relay and functions beyond the physical location as fixed, but it references other institutions, histories, and economies, as well as other sites and locations. Institutions such as Art Center College of Design, Norton Simon Museum, and Huntington Hospital also

perform as a condition or situation of site. The Henry Moore sculpture, as well as the body itself, all contribute to the matrix of "site" as situation that produced *Separated United Forms*. See Miwon Kwon, *One Place After Another: Site-Specific Art and Locational Identity* (Cambridge, Mass.: The MIT Press, 2002).

[6] I am humorously suggesting that scanning the Henry Moore with the imaging scanner would revive the Vital Life Force within in the sculpture. To generate such a fiction is to also suggest that the life force is inactive, or outdated, or did not exist to begin with; the vault of the Norton Simon Museum would then be seen to function as a resting place for the deceased. Once brought back to life, the sculpture is digitally transformed into a "binary large object" (also referred to as a B.L.O.B.); it has transformed from plop to blob. (Plop sculpture is a derogatory term for public sculpture that does not have any relationship to the site in which it is installed. Henry Moore was adamantly against developing any of his works towards a specific site.)

[7] Continuing with the fiction of the Vital Life Force being reanimated in *Reclining Form*: the sculpture continued to grow and divide as in a cellular meiosis—dividing from one form into two and then dividing again. The structure that I imposed onto the Henry Moore work is based on this idea of cellular division. The abstracted body of the Moore sculpture divided and rejoined generates a kinship between the two forms.

[8] The molds for the waxes were generated by manipulating the digital files that were originally created by the scanning process. The molds were milled out of plaster and foam. The process allowed for the omission of the full-scale pattern for the sculpture, privileging the digital workflow within the project, as well as reducing work done by handcrafted labor.
[9] Threaded through the entirety of this project is the integration and collaboration of physical and digital processes and the various labors associated with them.
[10] The public space that is created by the open landscaped area surrounding the site of the sculpture is complete with trees, benches, and sidewalks. I consider this to be an important addition, appropriating the conventions of outdoor modernist sculpture and its placement in and around architecture. There has been a long history of architects using figurative and abstract sculpture in and around modernist architecture and urban design. Alluding to a public and social space where people would gather spontaneously is an idea that can only happen in a situation where there is pedestrian activity. However, while this site is a hospital-oriented public site, very accessible by foot from many points, it functions mostly as a drive-by picture-window or as a set.

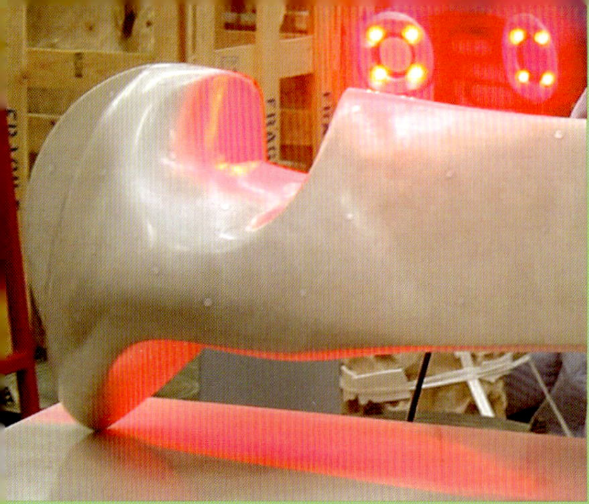

SAMPLING HENRY MOORE

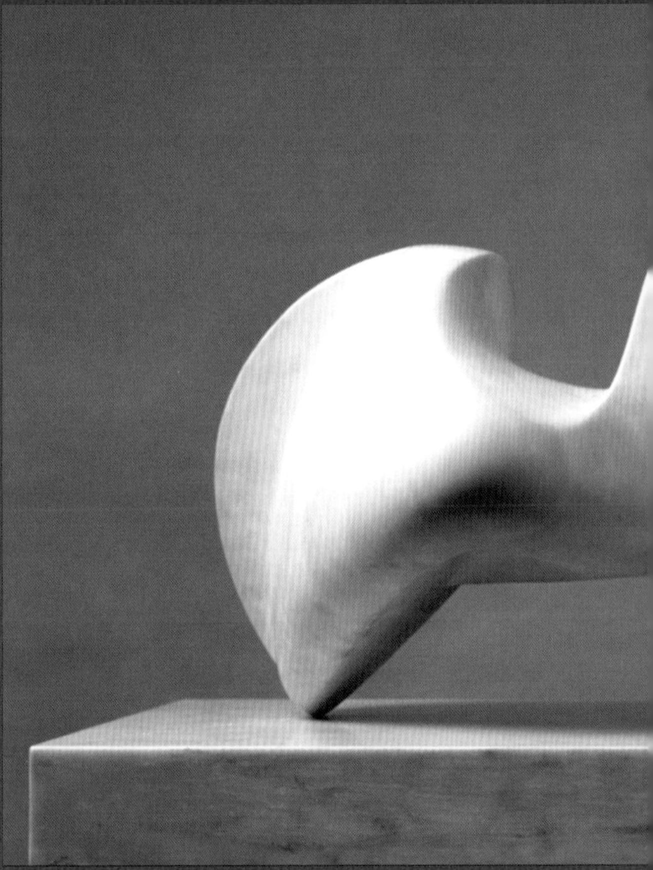

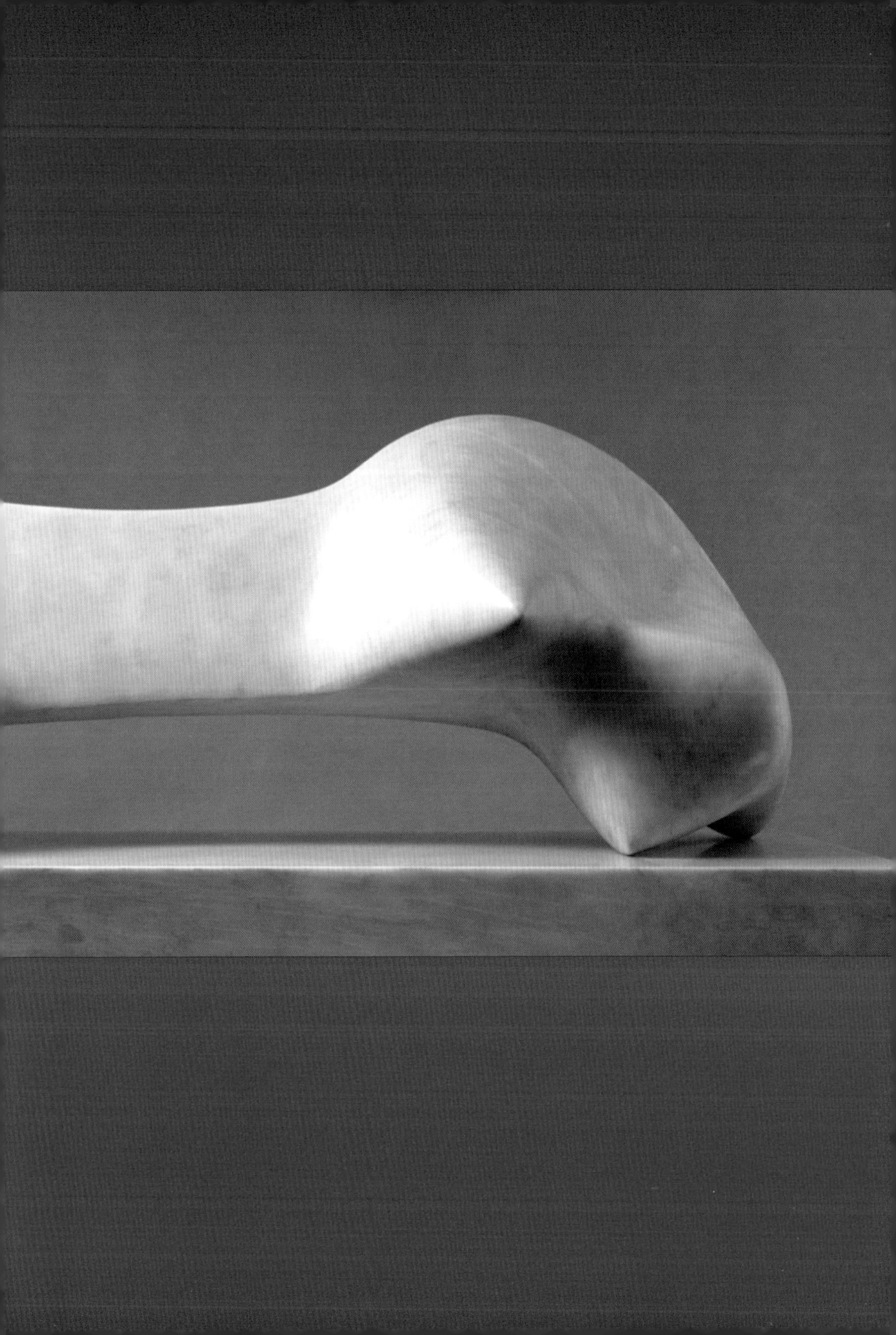

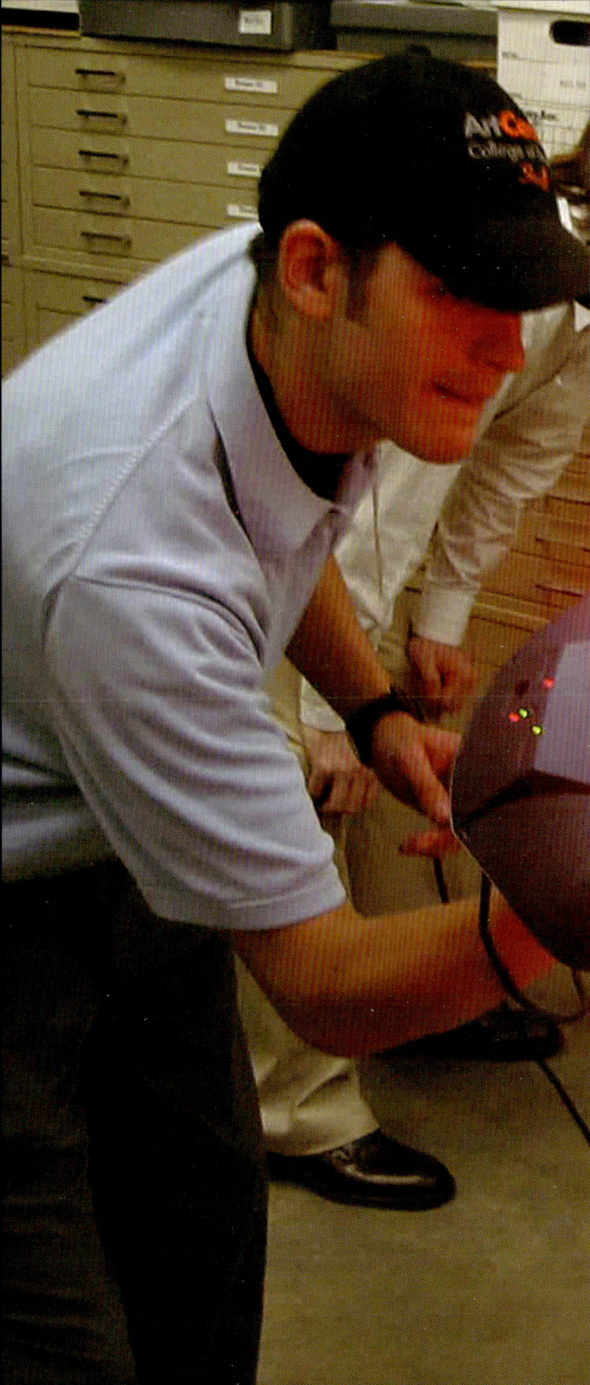

OCESS FOR THE
L DEVELOPMENT
ARATED UNITED
STARTED WITH
AN DATA THAT
TRIEVED FROM
SCANNING
ION ON THE
MOORE SCULPTURE
NORTON SIMON
. THE SCAN DATA
N AS A POINT
OR POINTS
D IN XYZ SPACE.
WAS THEN
TED FROM THE
CLOUD.

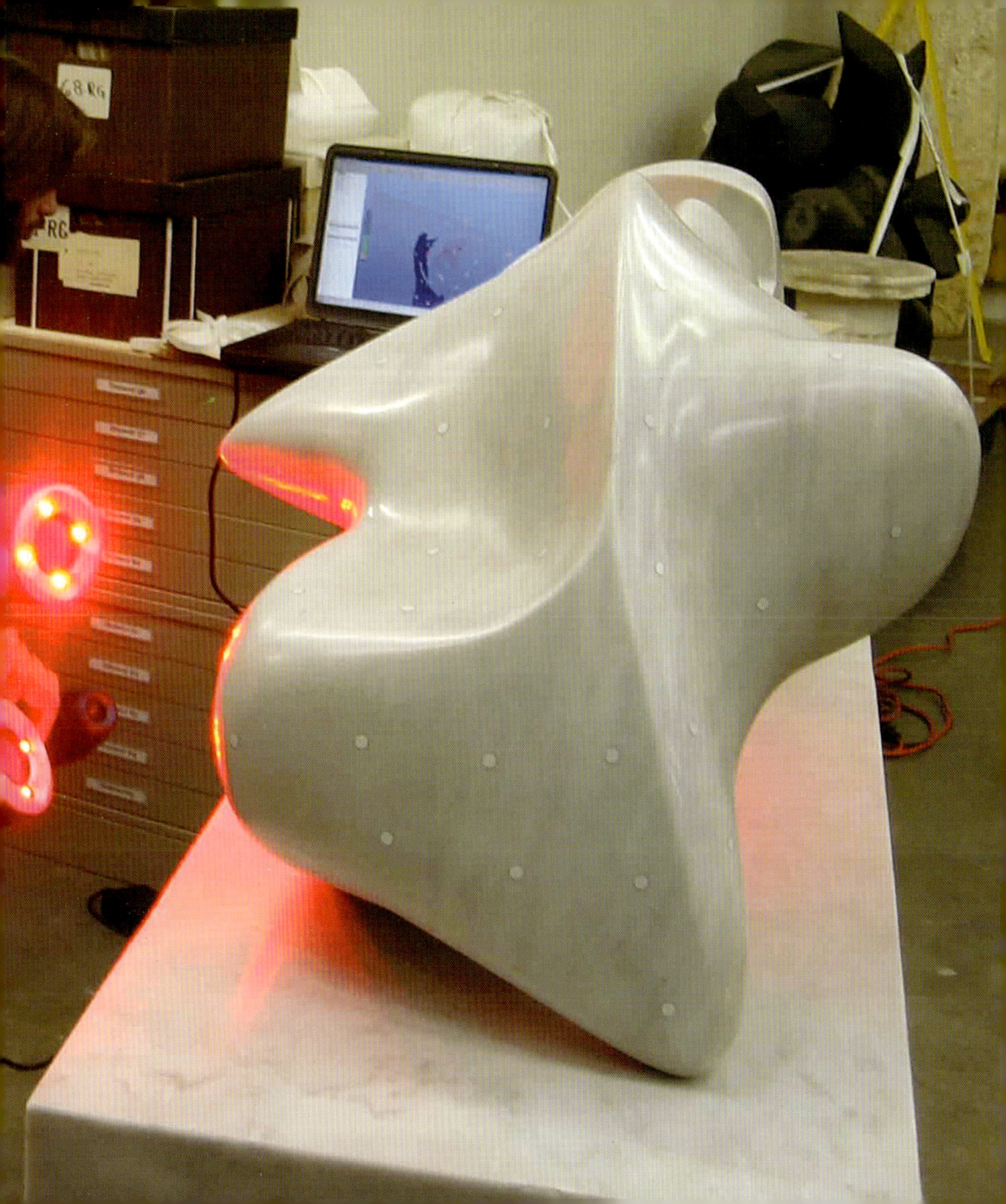

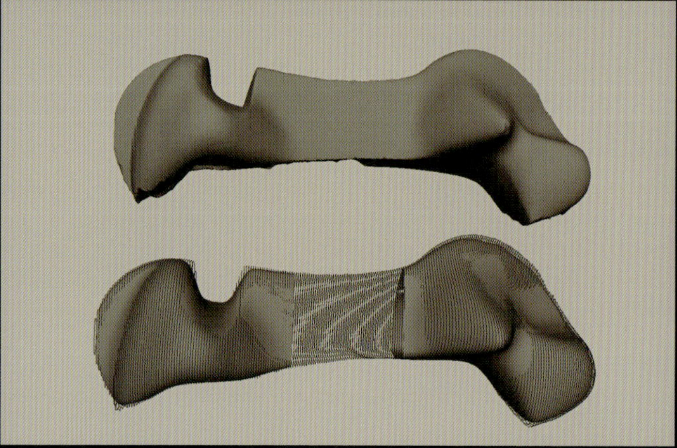

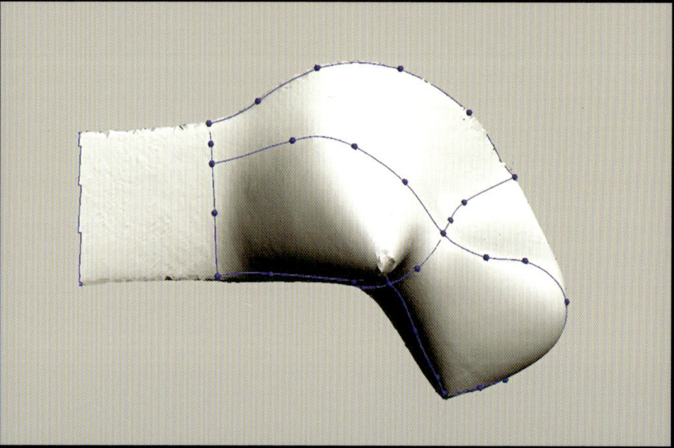

FROM THE POINT CLOUD, A MESH OF TRIANGULATED POINTS (VERTICES) WAS MADE THAT IS CONNECTED BY

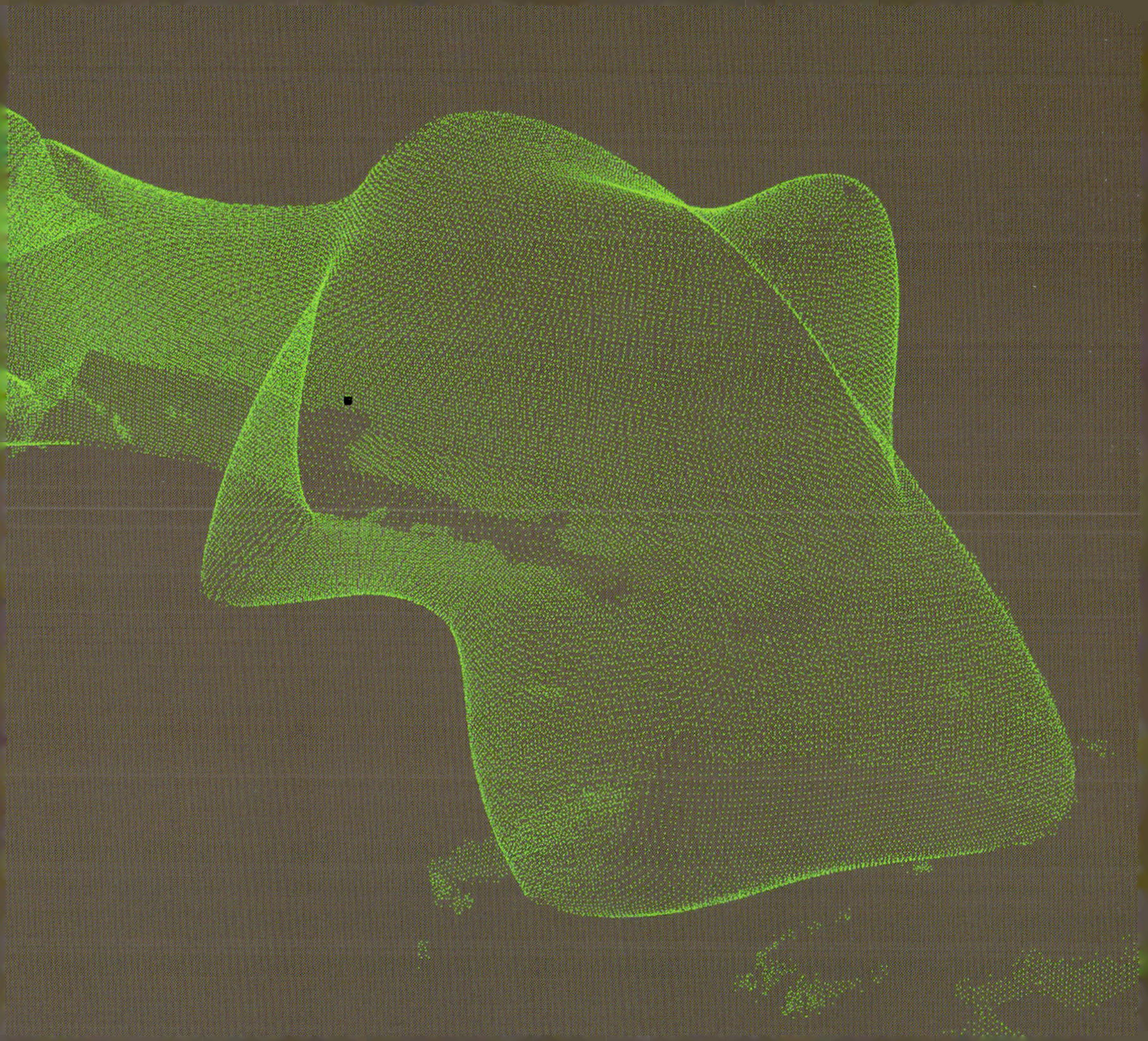

Curves (slices) were generated over the entire model and a nurbs surface was lofted. The topology was then reformulated and the surfaces arranged to best represent the forms. This required the creation of a patch model, or several individual and continuous surfaces acting as one blanket and giving the illusion of a complete volume.

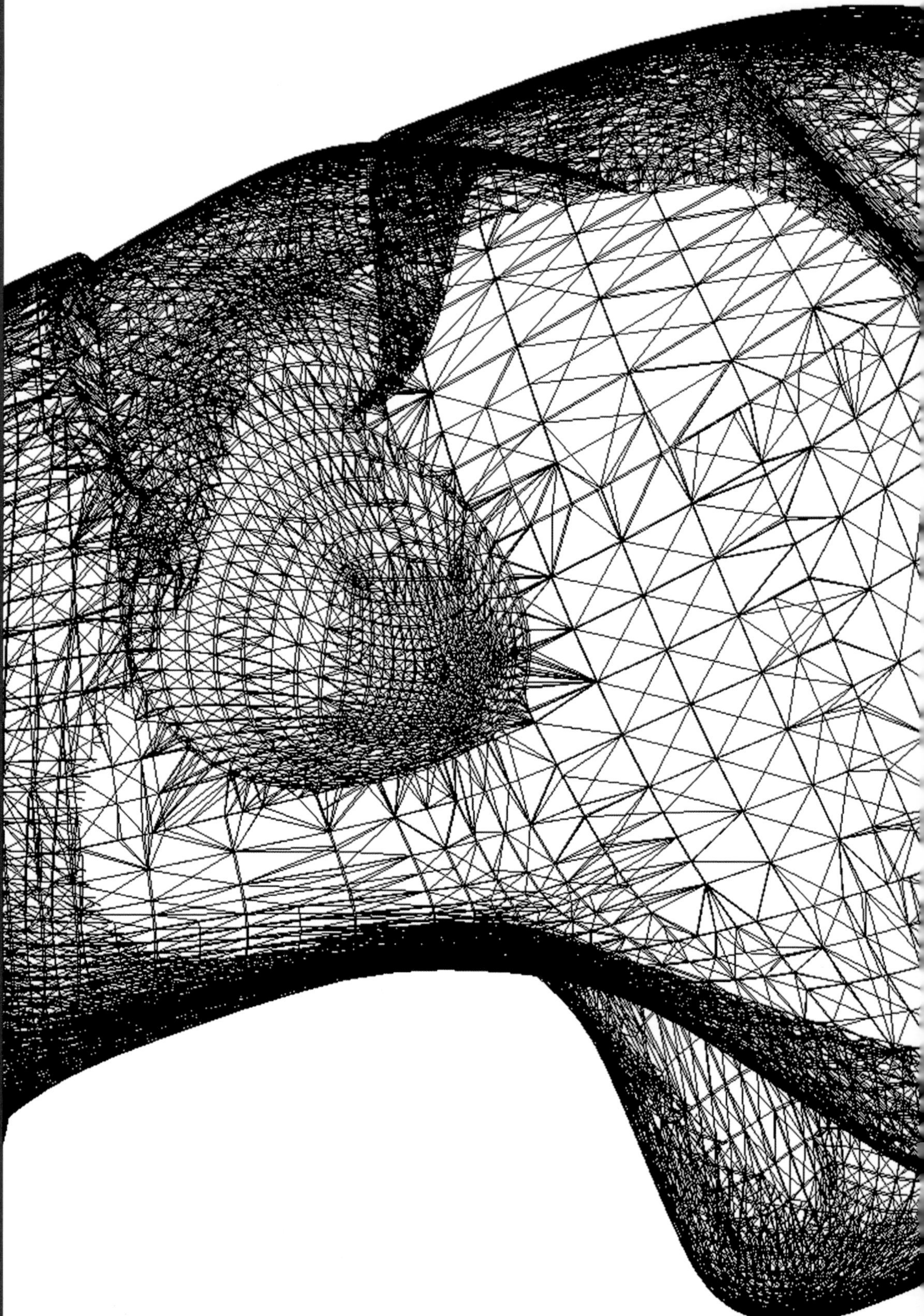

Once the reverse engineering was completed, the separated forms were developed to produce two parts. This was achieved by sculpting the control points of the NURBS surfaces to manipulate and finesse their shapes. Once the two parts were complete, experimentation continued with how to unite them again. At first, experimentation with deforming the parts was initiated. Then, it was decided to keep the parts intact, but simply generate permutations with simple rotations and translations. A taxonomy of these variations were produced and from that a basic logic was applied, which is to flip front and back and transform right to left. This operation produced the final *Separated United Forms*.

These parts, which are in essence doubled or superimposed, were then united digitally with a boolean function to join them into a singular and manufacturable object.

Jason Pilarski

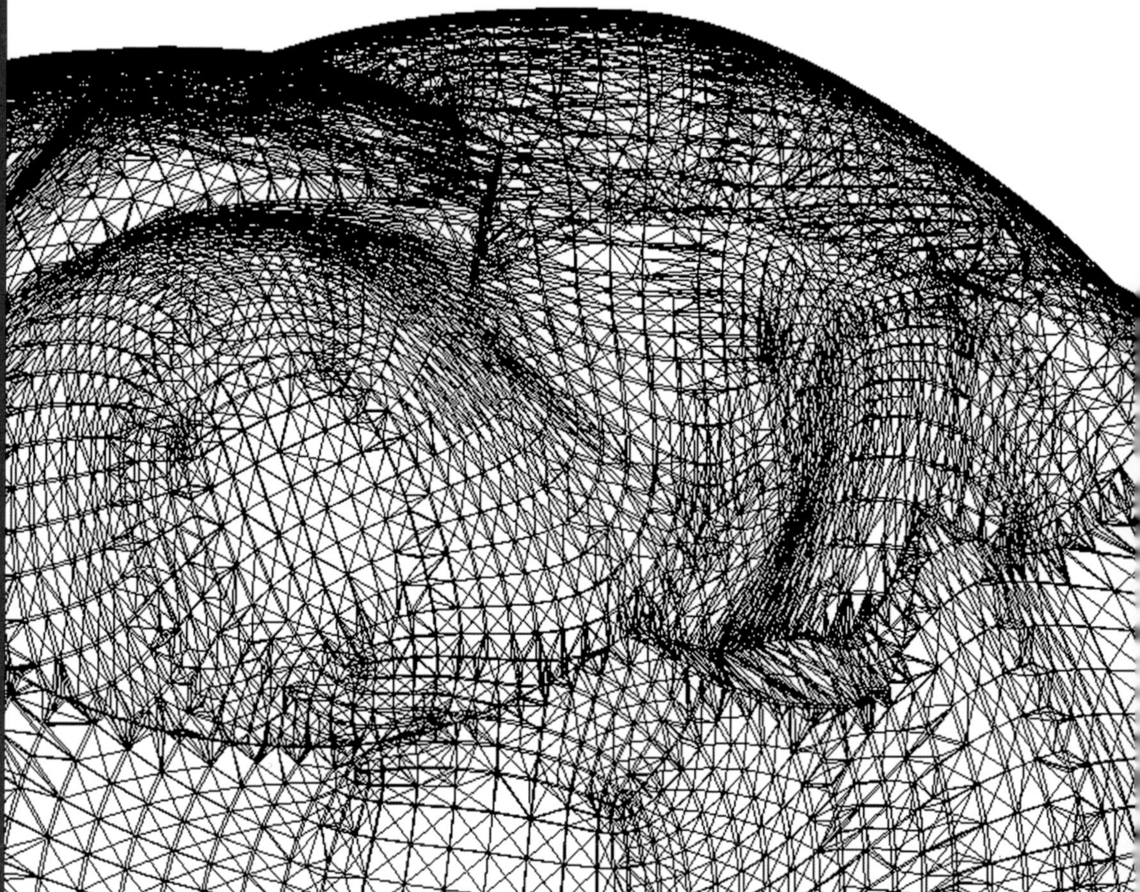

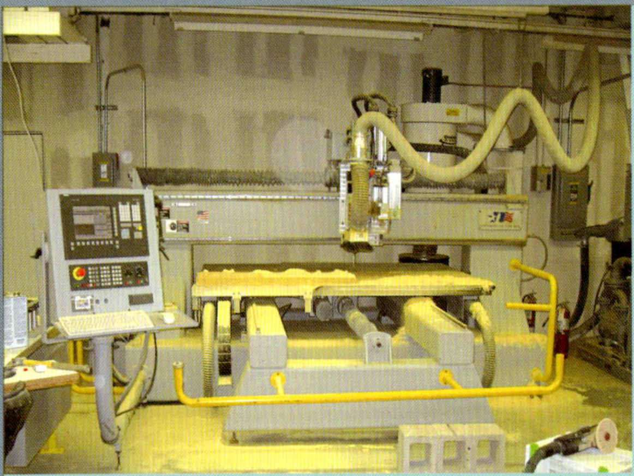

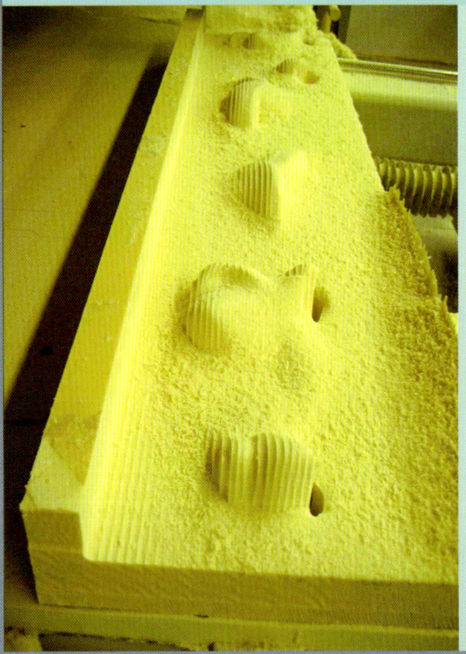

MODELS

The application of models, both digital and physical, on *Separated United Forms* enabled a remarkably complete understanding of form, facture, materiality, and cost. They provided a place to consider and ultimately to manage a project of this scale with considerable confidence. Perhaps their most important function on this project was to serve as a rather sensitive design tool, allowing for an agile means to identify and flesh out the sculpture with each successive iteration.

The models were produced in ten-pound density urethane foam, which is a common material used for prototyping and for proofing tooling settings. The models were output at a scale of one inch to one foot, which helped establish a common architectural relationship to scale. They were CNC- [computer numerical control] machined at Machine Histories in Los Angeles, California, using a Northwood 3 axis router. The parts were machined in halves according to the four-inch thickness of the material. Epoxy, bondo, and polyester primer were used to adhere the pieces together, fill in any seams, and smooth out the toolmarks left by the machining process. The plinth was also modeled in order to factor in the details surrounding this significant component of the sculpture. The divisions within the plinth, along with the placement of the lighting and the location of the sculptures, were more easily evaluated with an analogue version of the data.

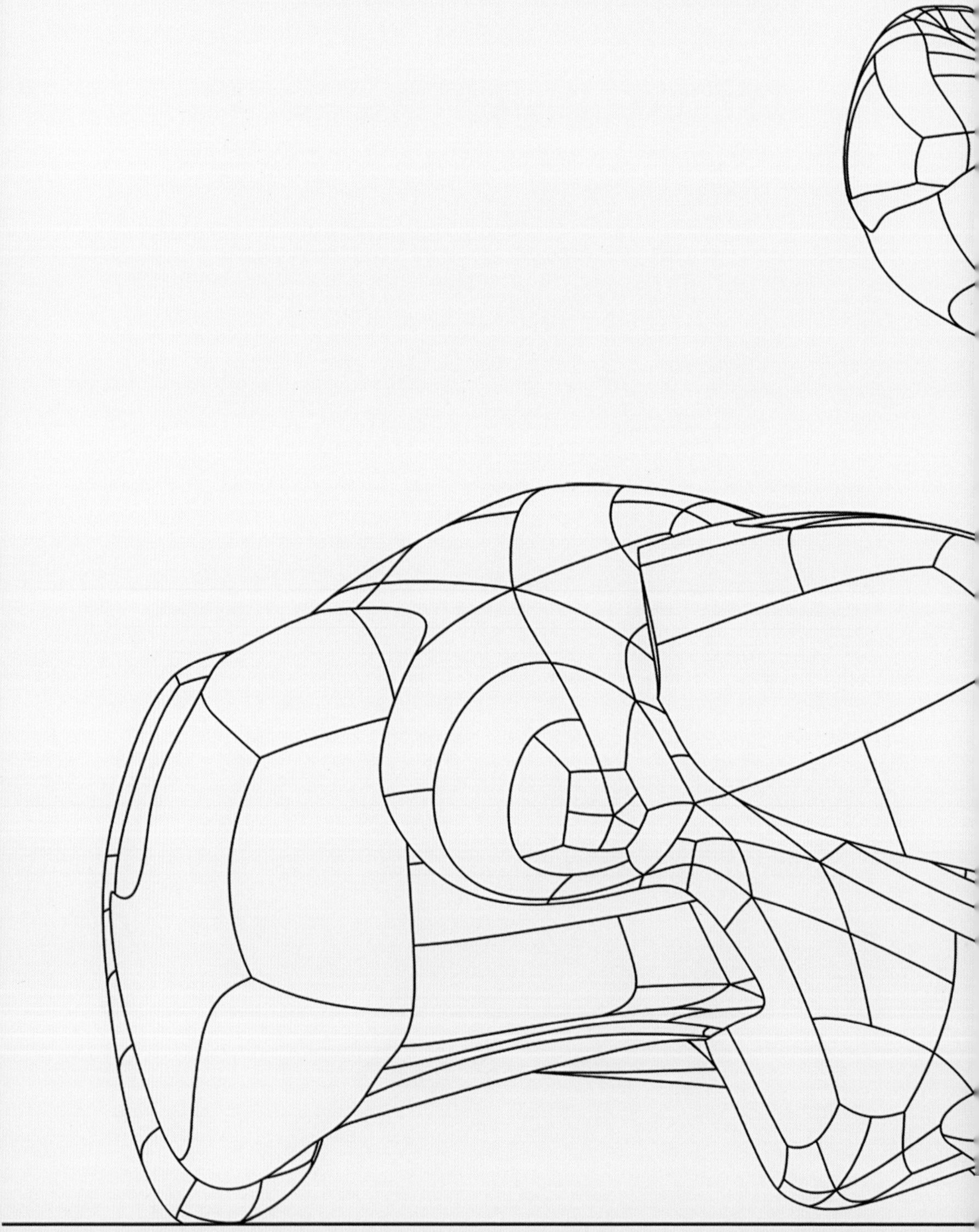

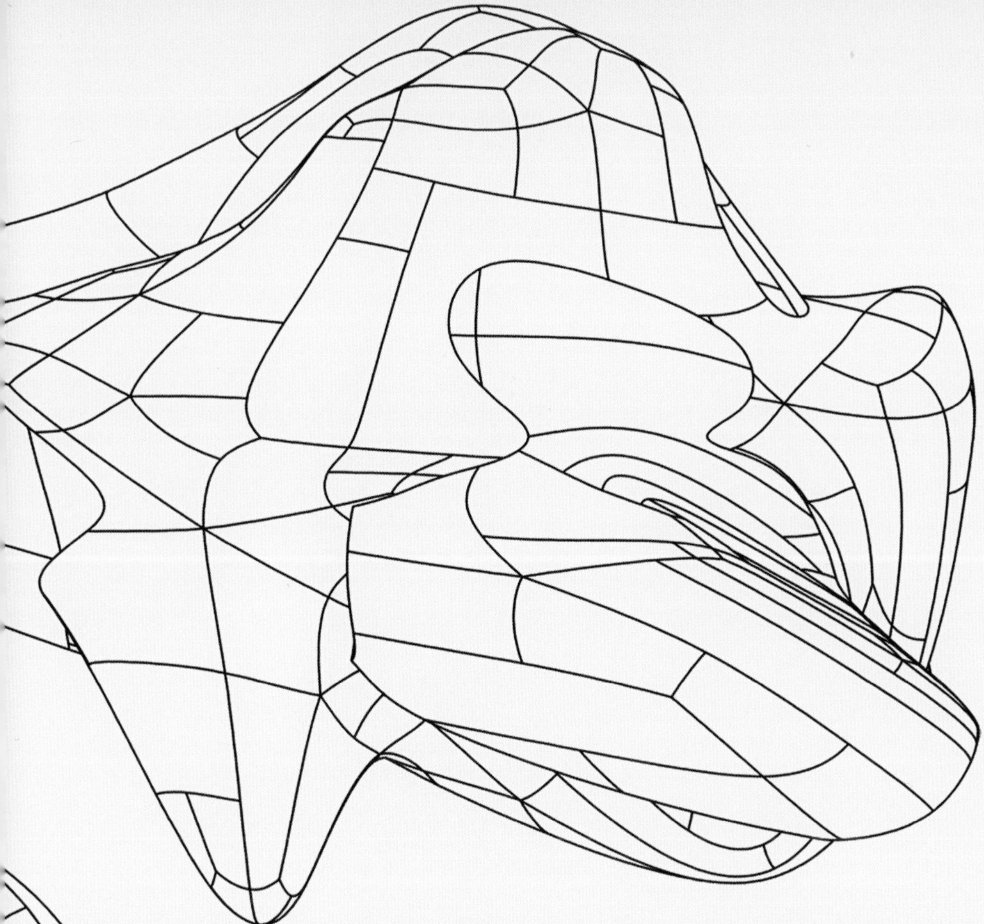

While renderings were made using Mental Ray (a rendering software program), it was far easier to properly address the finish of the pieces in their physical state. The renderings did, however, provide an accurate means to consider the quality of the forms being generated, as well as facilitating editing and refinement. There were aspects of the initial sculpture that seem to have been influenced more by product design of that time than by the human form. The fact that the pieces were dissected into two main parts also meant that those lines and that form language had to be maintained to complete or perhaps cap off the now cut-open ends of the sculpture. Without a high-end rendering tool to properly display the highlights and continuity of the surfaces created, it would have been difficult to recreate the perfect smoothness found in the original piece, which is more easily achieved through hand-sculpting.

Jason Pilarski

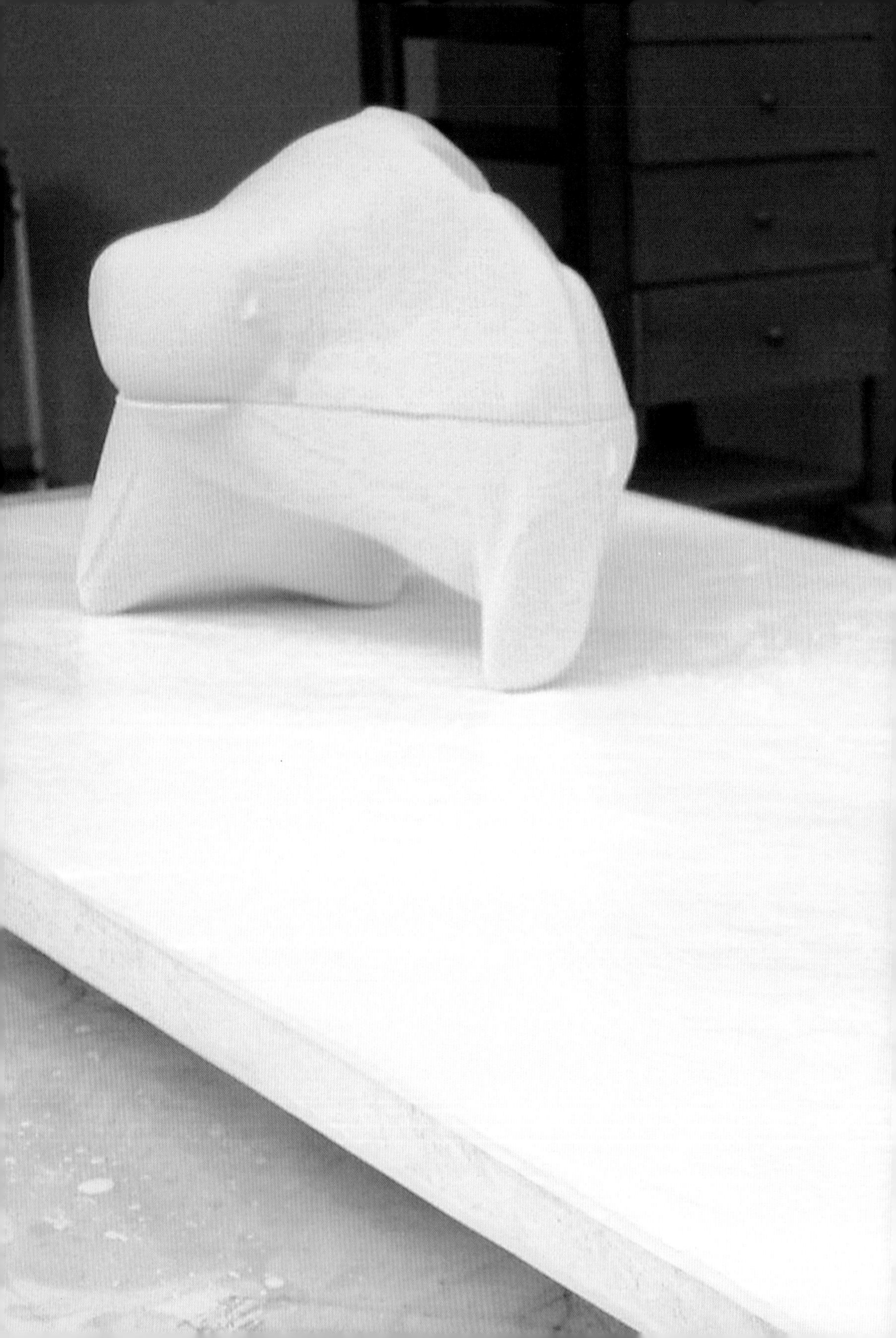

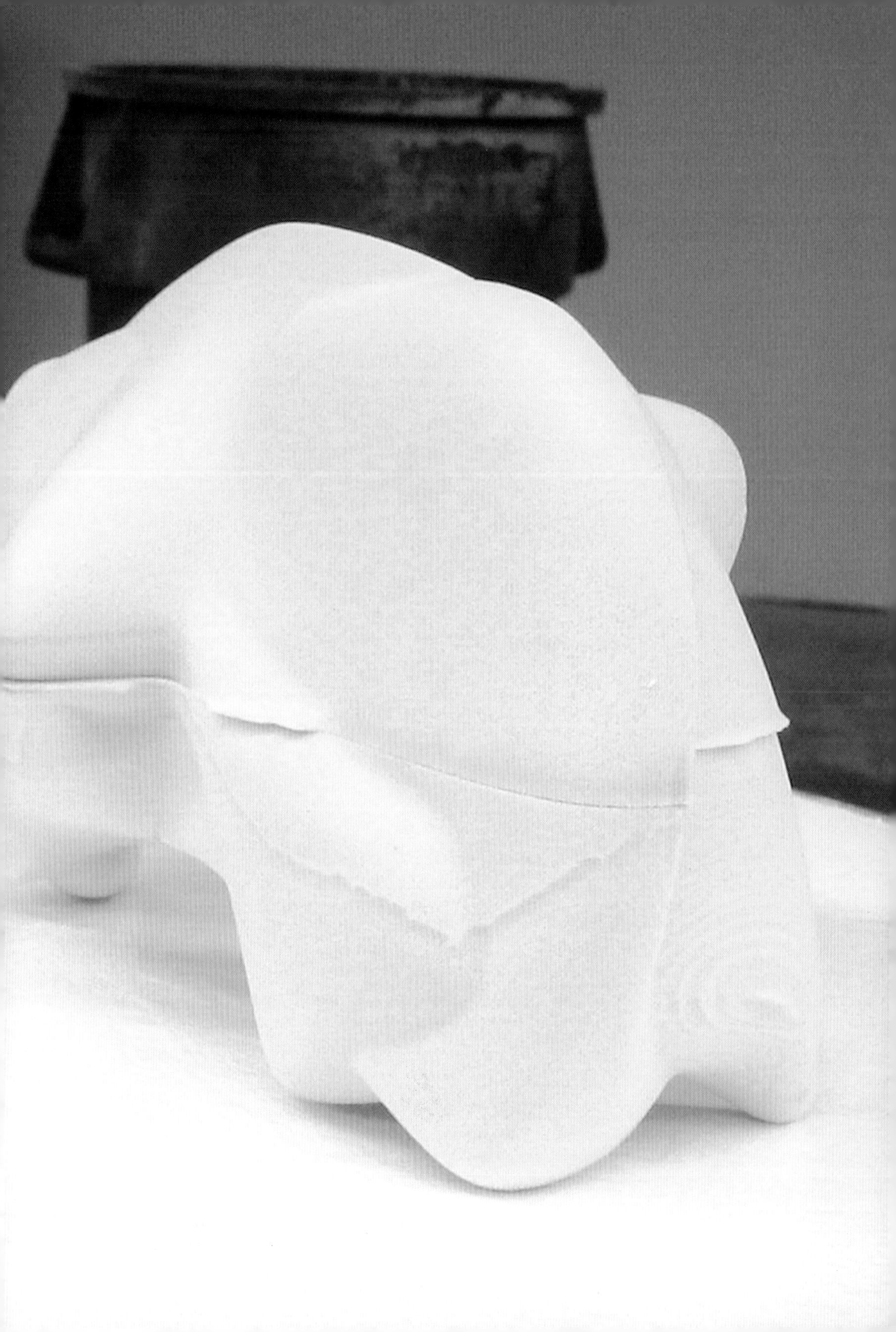

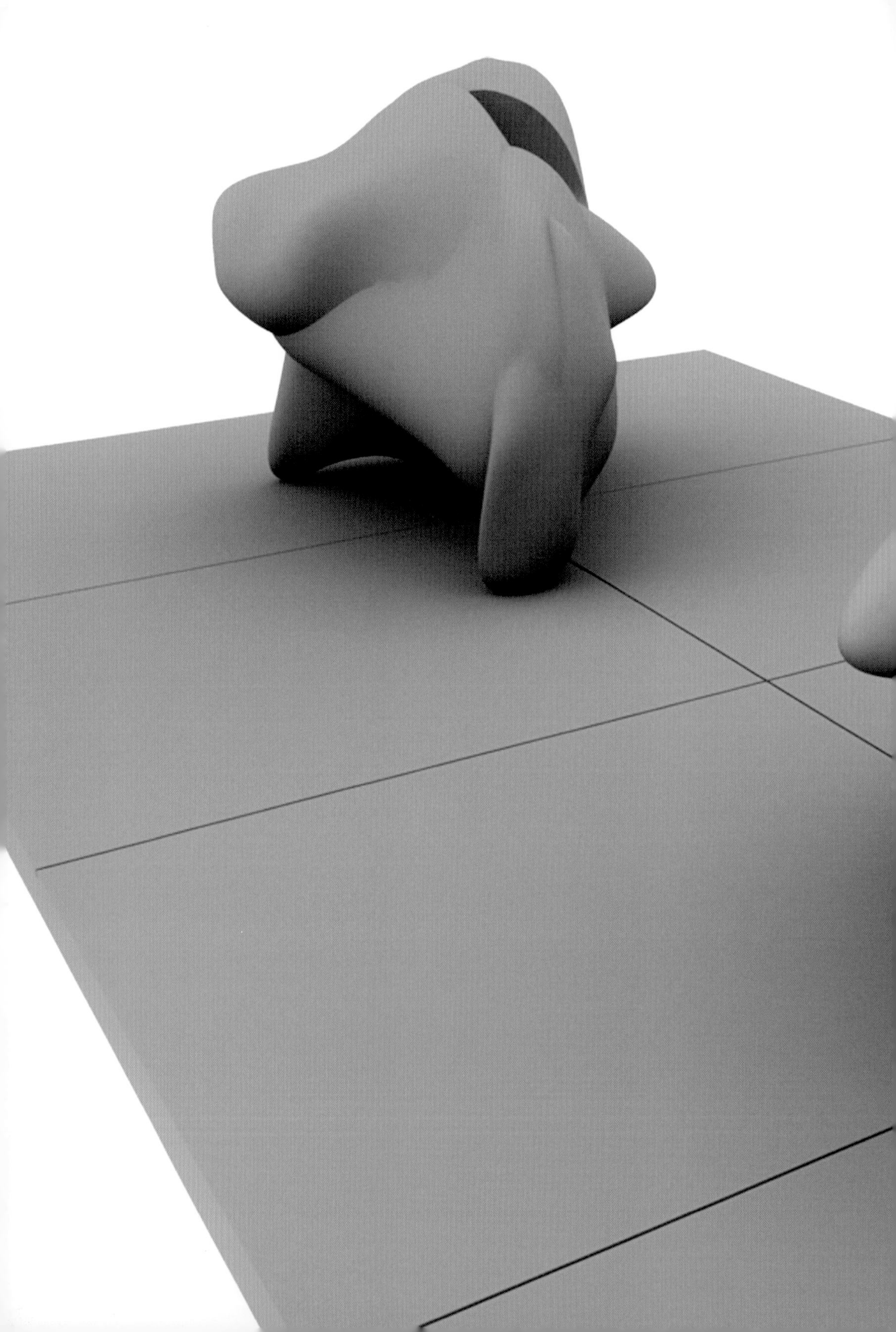

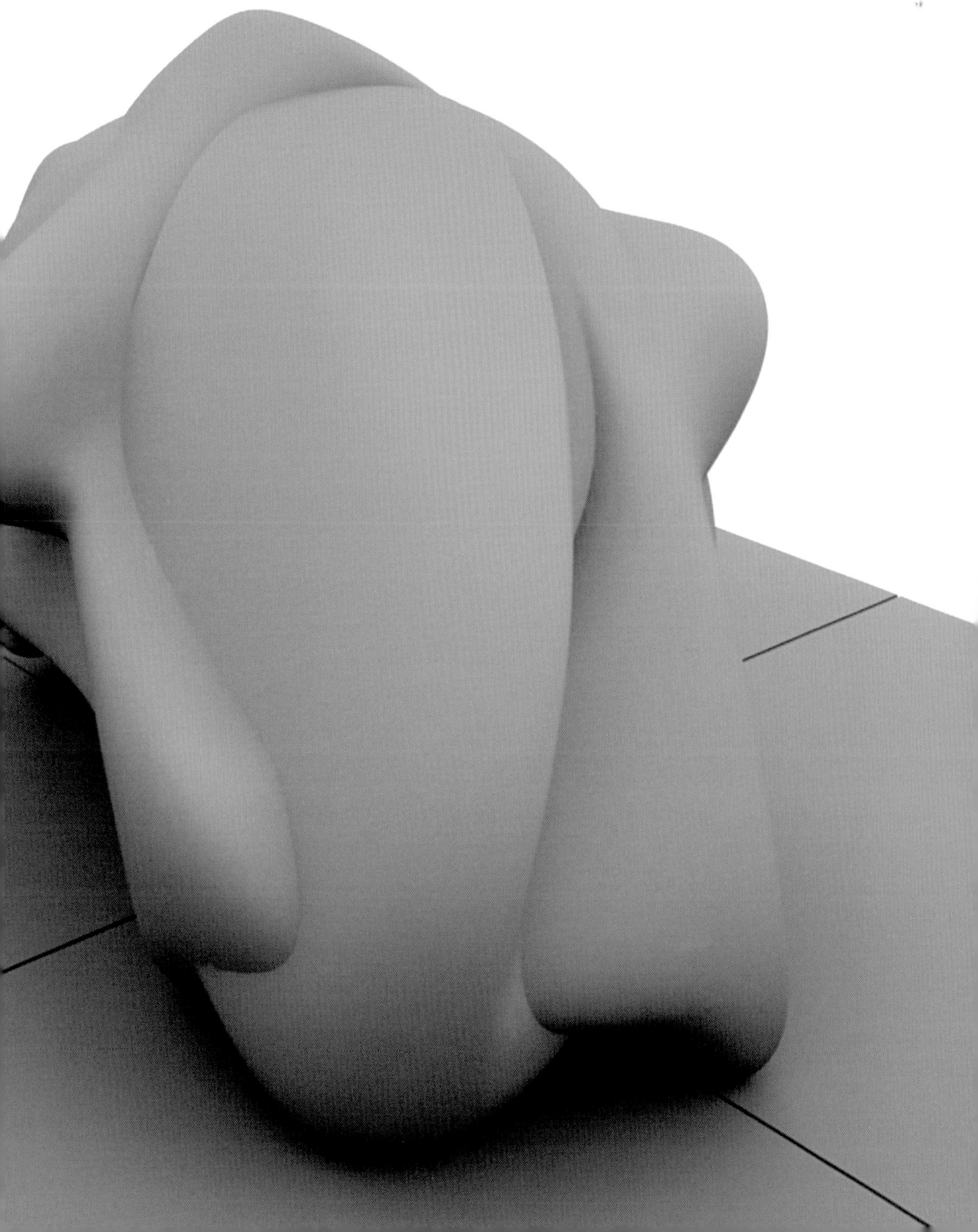

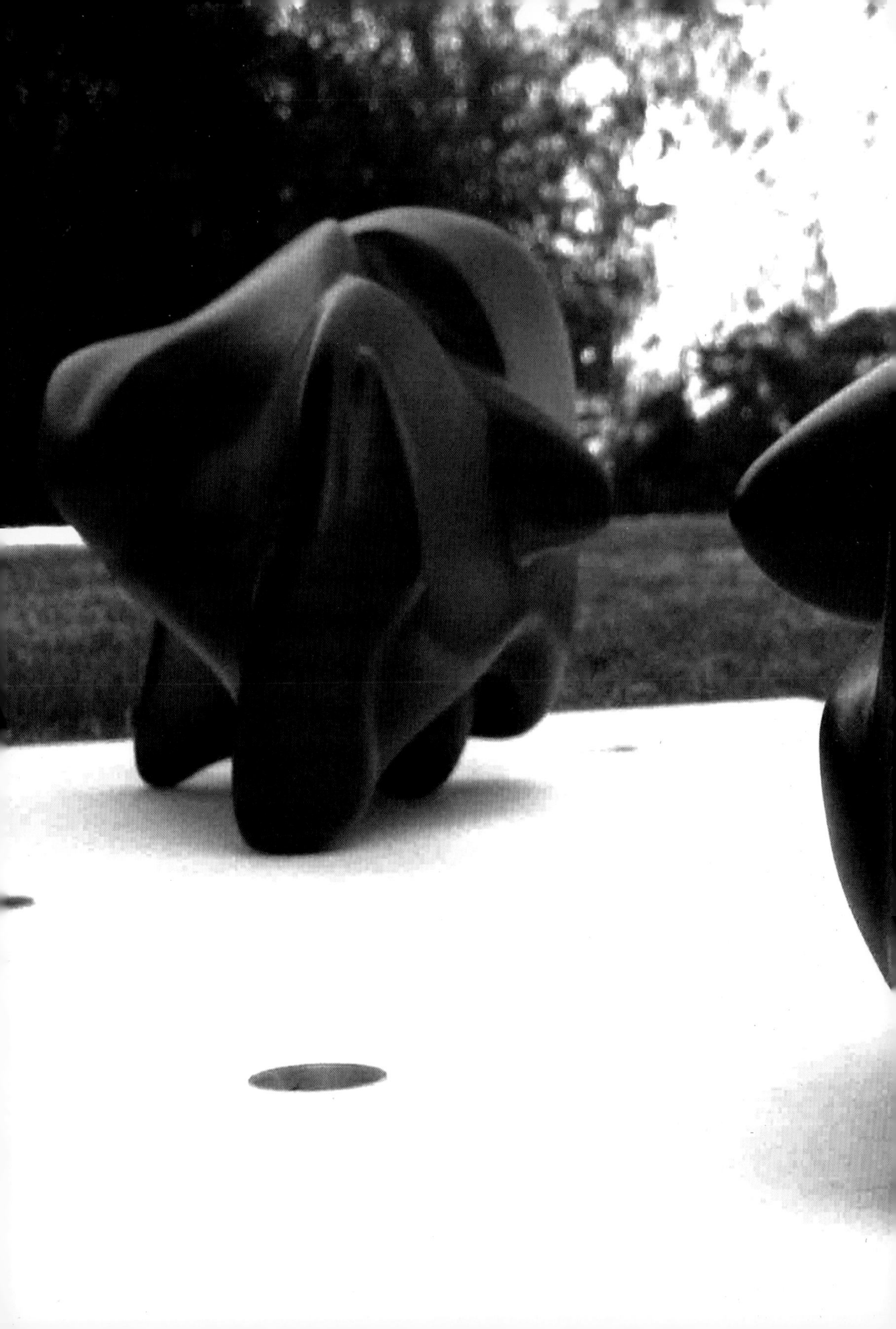

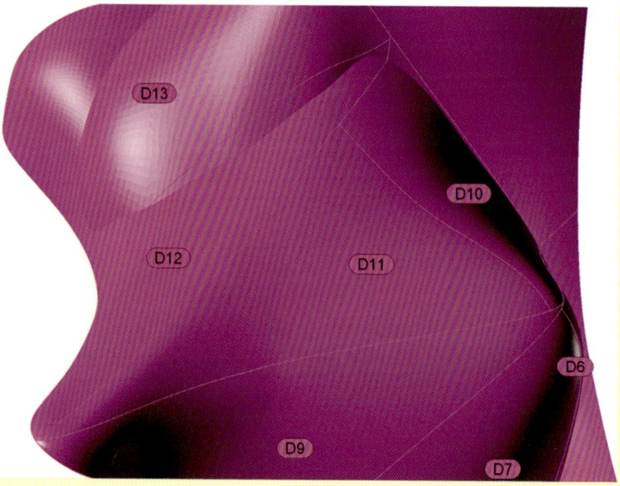
D13
D10
D12
D11
D6
D9
D7

SECTIONING

The 3D SUF computer model was sectioned into panels that were sized to fit in the ceramic shell tank, which is roughly 30 inches by 30 inches. Sectioning was also performed based on accessible geometry, i.e. working around undercuts, the goal being to achieve the flattest patterns with the least change in depth. All of this was executed in Rhino, a commercial nurbs-based 3D modeling tool.

Dylan Farnum

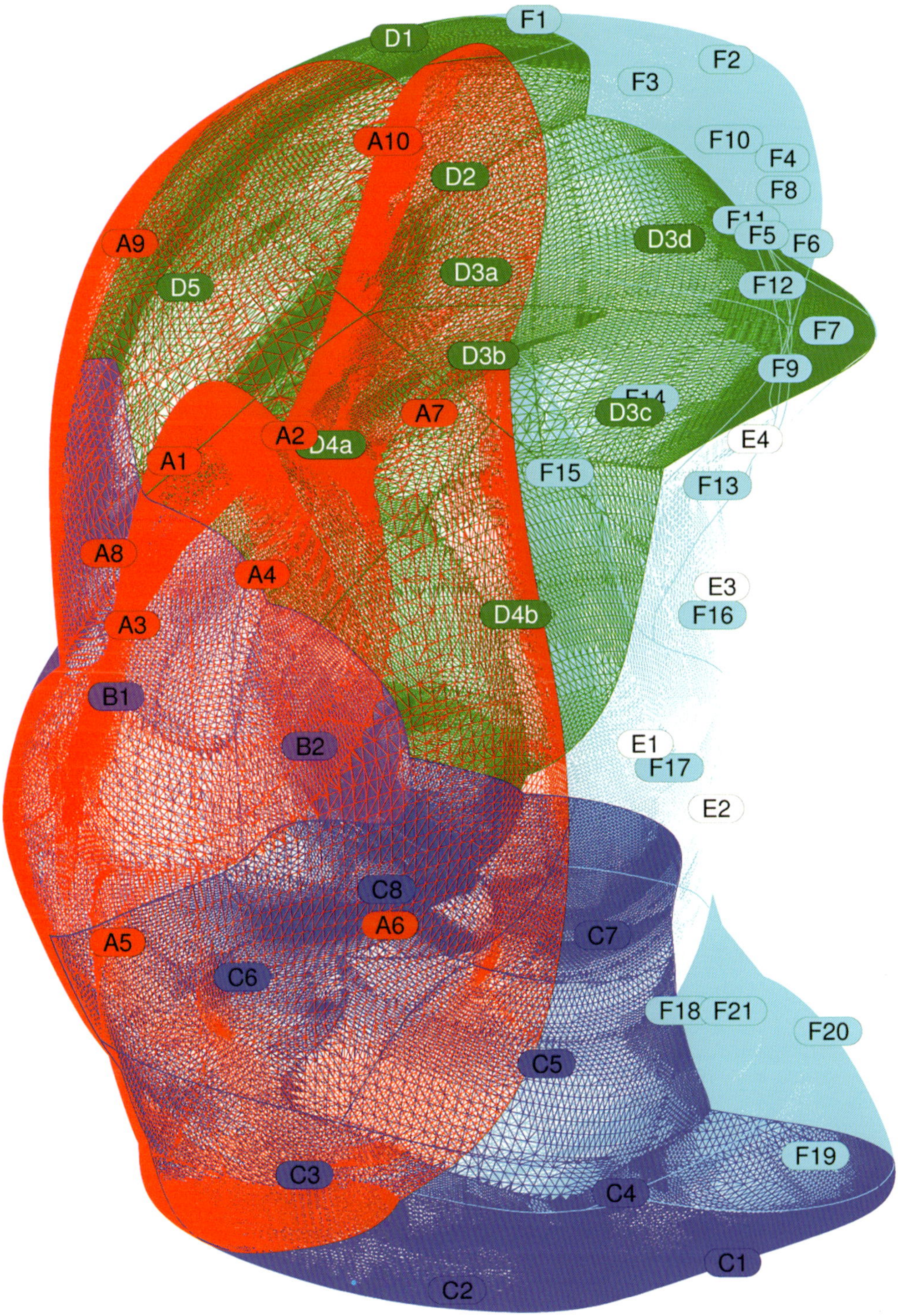
F1
D1
F2
F3
A10
F10
F4
D2
F8
F11
F5
D3d
F6
A9
D3a
D5
F12
F7
D3b
F9
F14
A7
D3c
A2
D4a
E4
A1
F15
F13
A8
A4
E3
D4b
F16
A3
B1
B2
E1
F17
E2
C8
A6
C7
A5
C6
F18
F21
F20
C5
F19
C3
C4
C1
C2

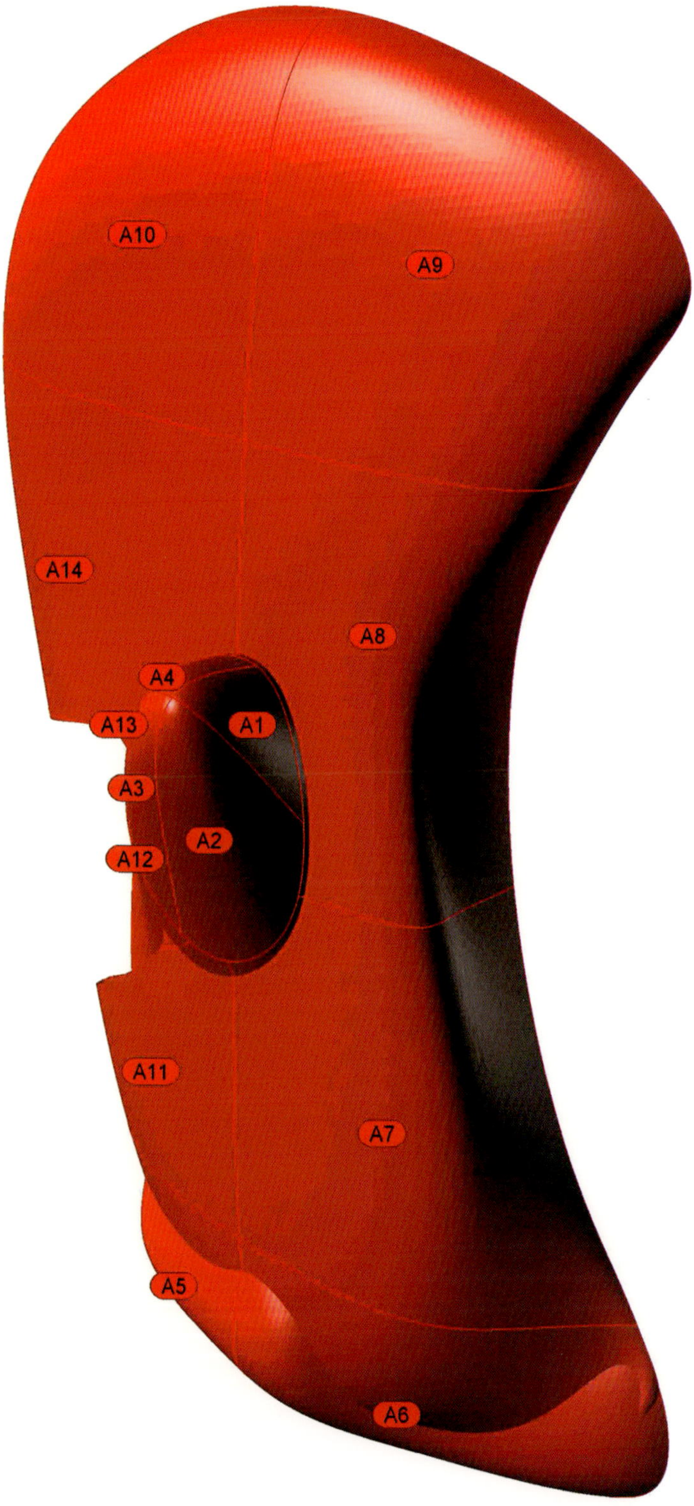
A10
A9
A14
A8
A4
A13
A1
A3
A2
A12
A11
A7
A5
A6

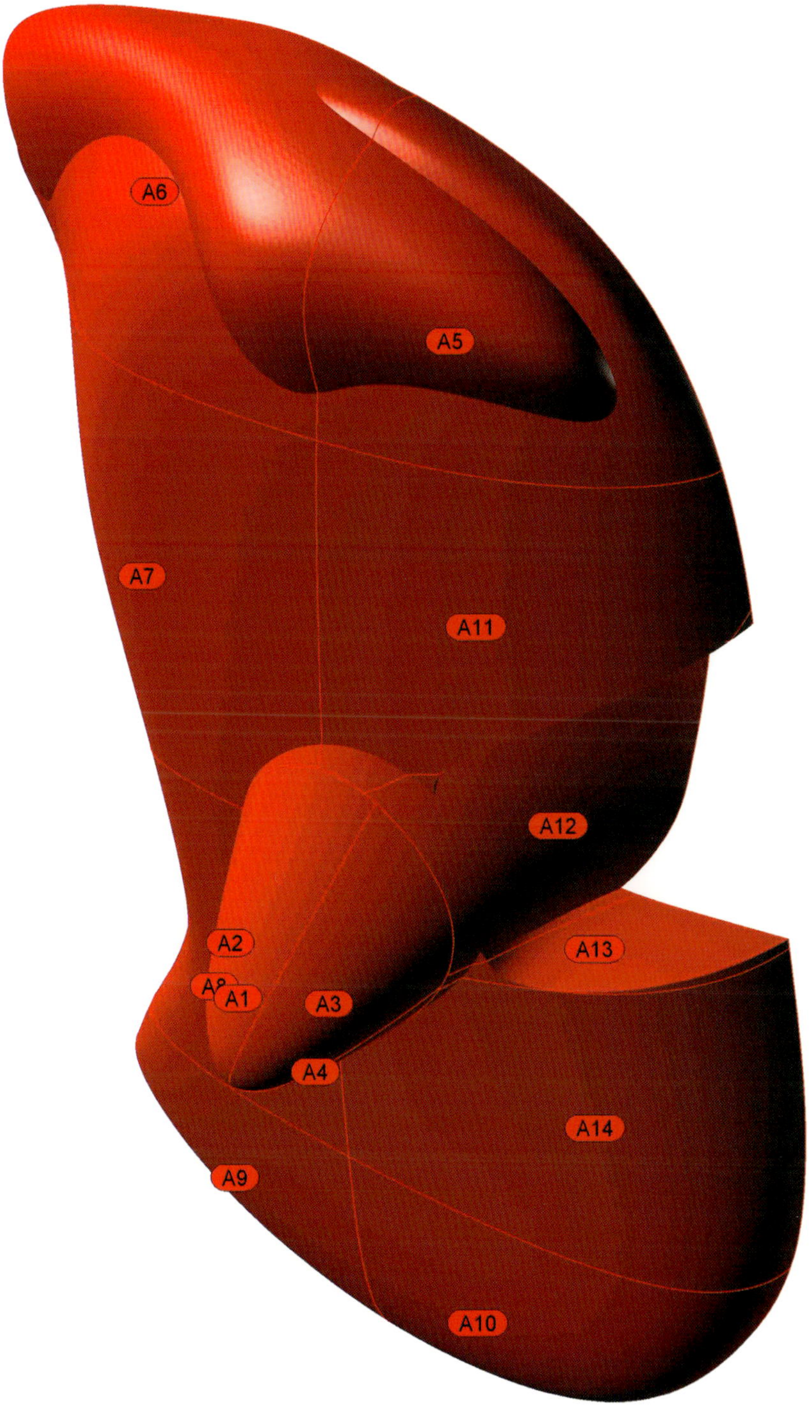
A6
A5
A7
A11
A12
A2
A13
A8
A1
A3
A4
A14
A9
A10

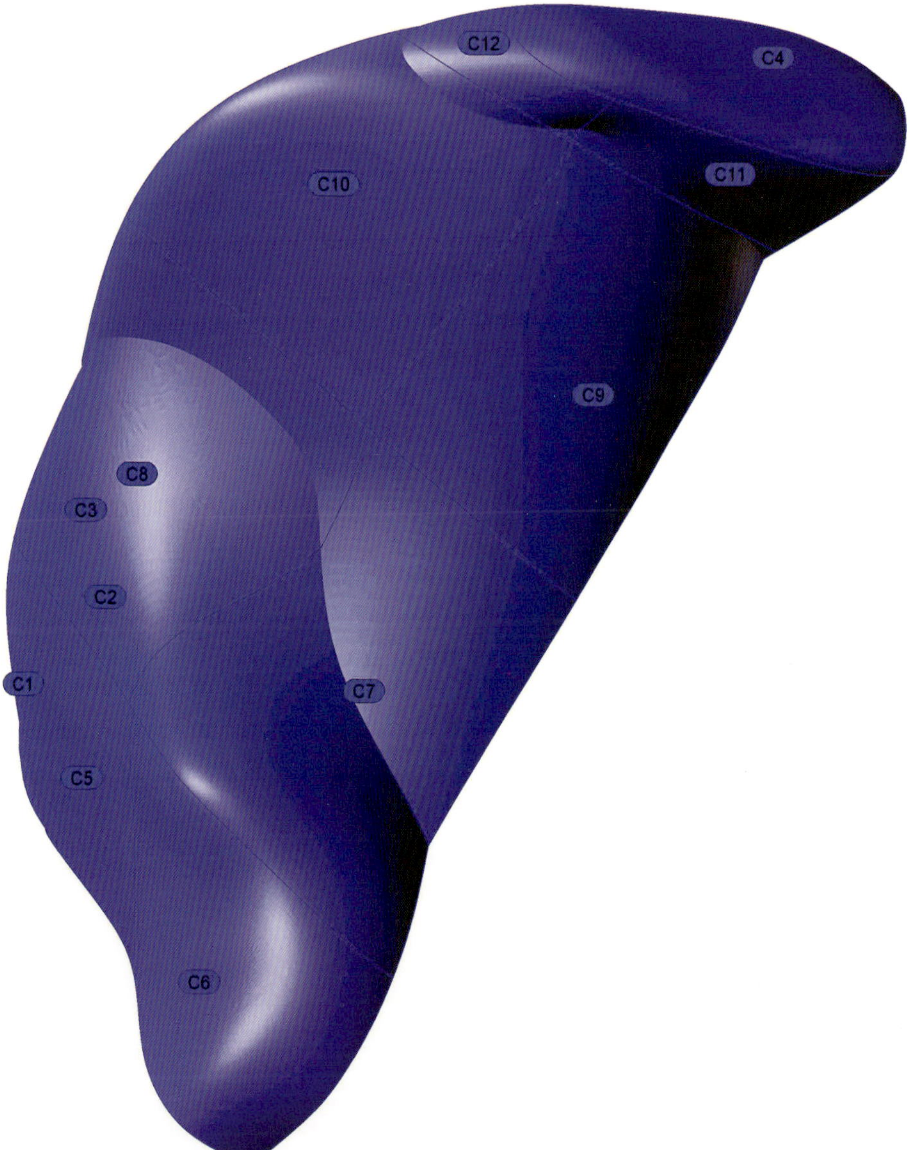
C12
C4
C10
C11
C9
C8
C3
C2
C1
C7
C5
C6

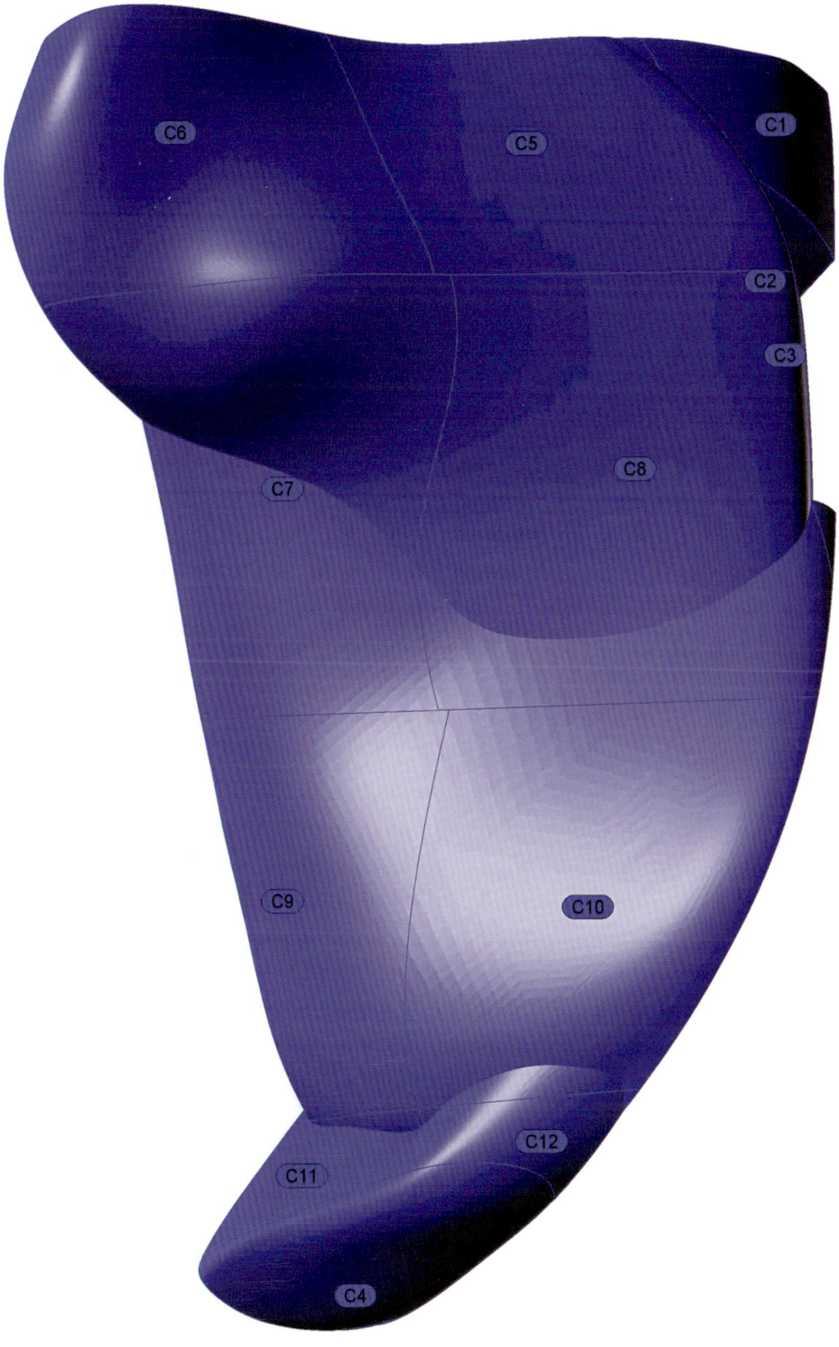
C6
C5
C1
C2
C3
C7
C8
C9
C10
C12
C11
C4

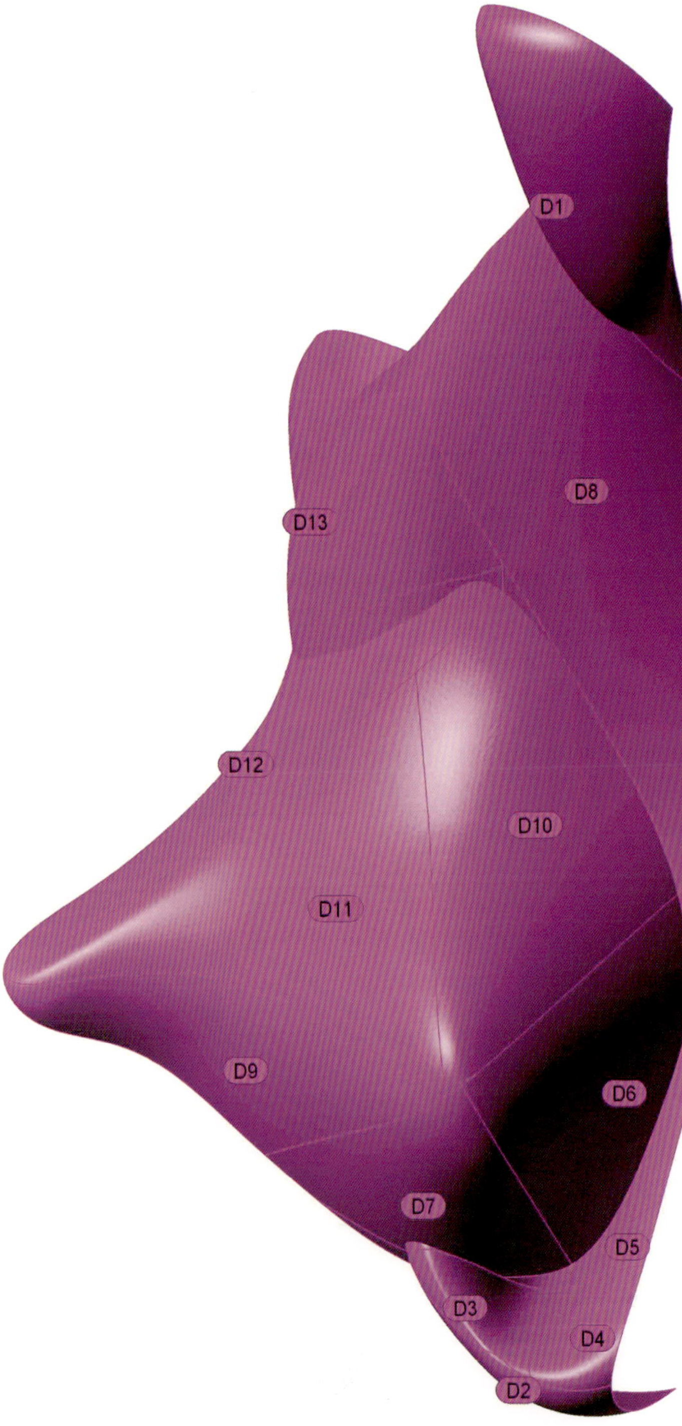
D1
D8
D13
D12
D10
D11
D9
D6
D7
D5
D3
D4
D2

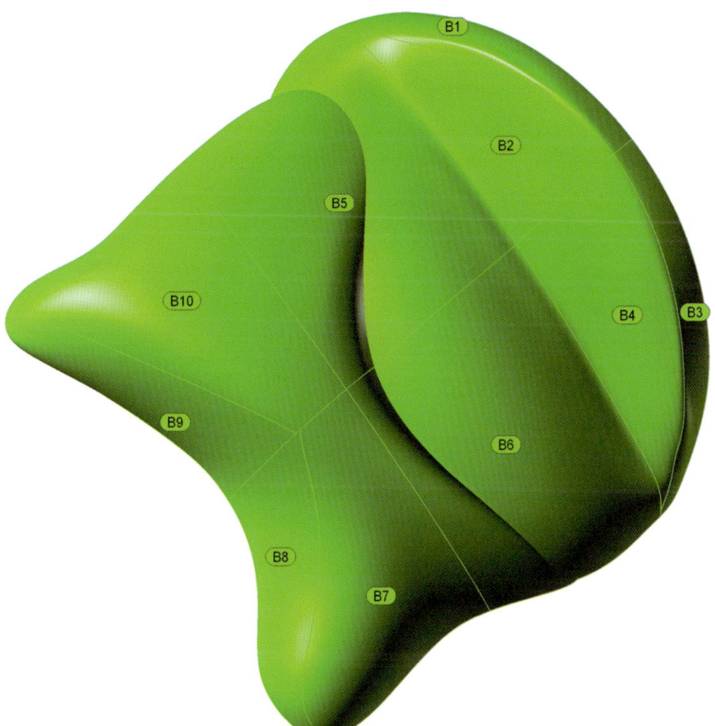
B1
B2
B5
B10
B4
B3
B9
B6
B8
B7

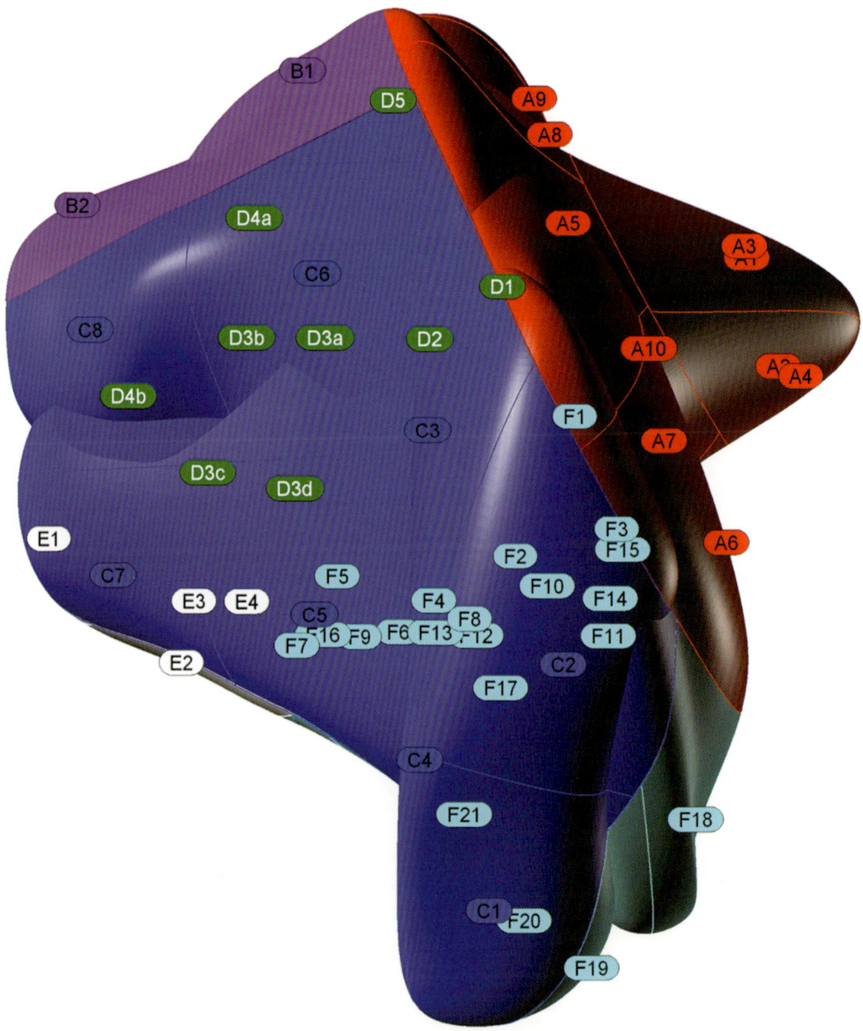
B1
D5
A9
A8
B2
D4a
A5
A3
C6
D1
C8
D3b
D3a
D2
A10
A4
D4b
F1
C3
A7
D3c
D3d
F3
F15
A6
E1
F2
C7
F5
F10
E3
E4
F4
F14
C5
F8
F16
F9
F6
F13
F12
F11
F7
E2
C2
F17
C4
F21
F18
C1
F20
F19

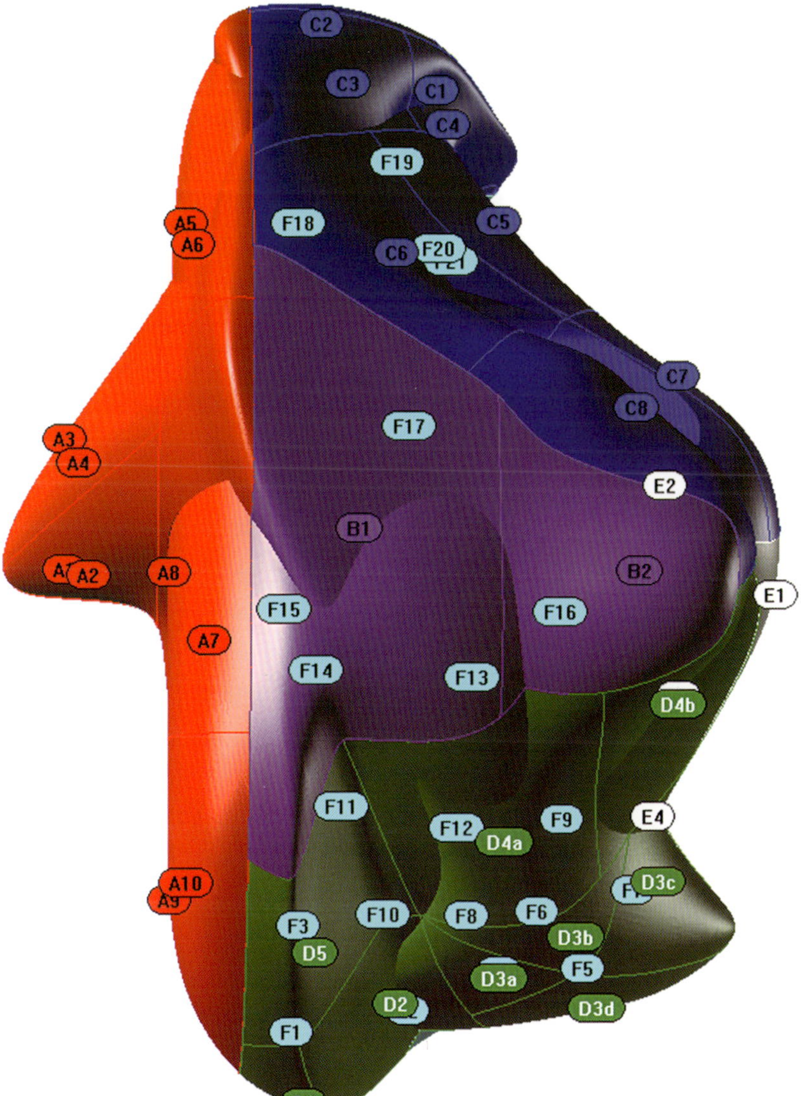
C2
C3
C1
C4
F19
A5
A6
F18
C5
C6
F20
C7
C8
F17
A3
A4
E2
B1
B2
A2
A8
E1
F15
F16
A7
F14
F13
D4b
F11
F12
F9
E4
D4a
A10
D3c
F3
F10
F8
F6
D3b
D5
F5
D3a
D2
D3d
F1
D1

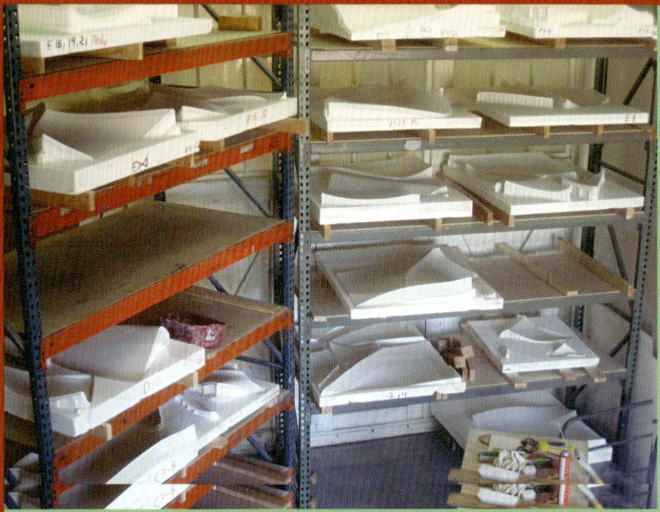

MOLDS/ WAXES

The forms were divided into panels and the geometry was inverted. The negative pattern, or mold was then milled out in vacuum cast plaster. The vacuumed plaster provided a beautiful and flawless substrate from which wax patterns could be pulled with very little additional hand work being required. There are two key technological innovations within this methodology: the first being the milling of plaster (a near perfect combination of high quality material at a relatively low cost), the second being the direct milling of the molds from a digital model. A significant amount of time was saved by avoiding the necessity of carving an original and then pulling a rubber mold, in order to cast the wax patterns. Unusual to these types of projects, the sculptures never existed as complete physical forms until they were cast in bronze.

Dylan Farnum

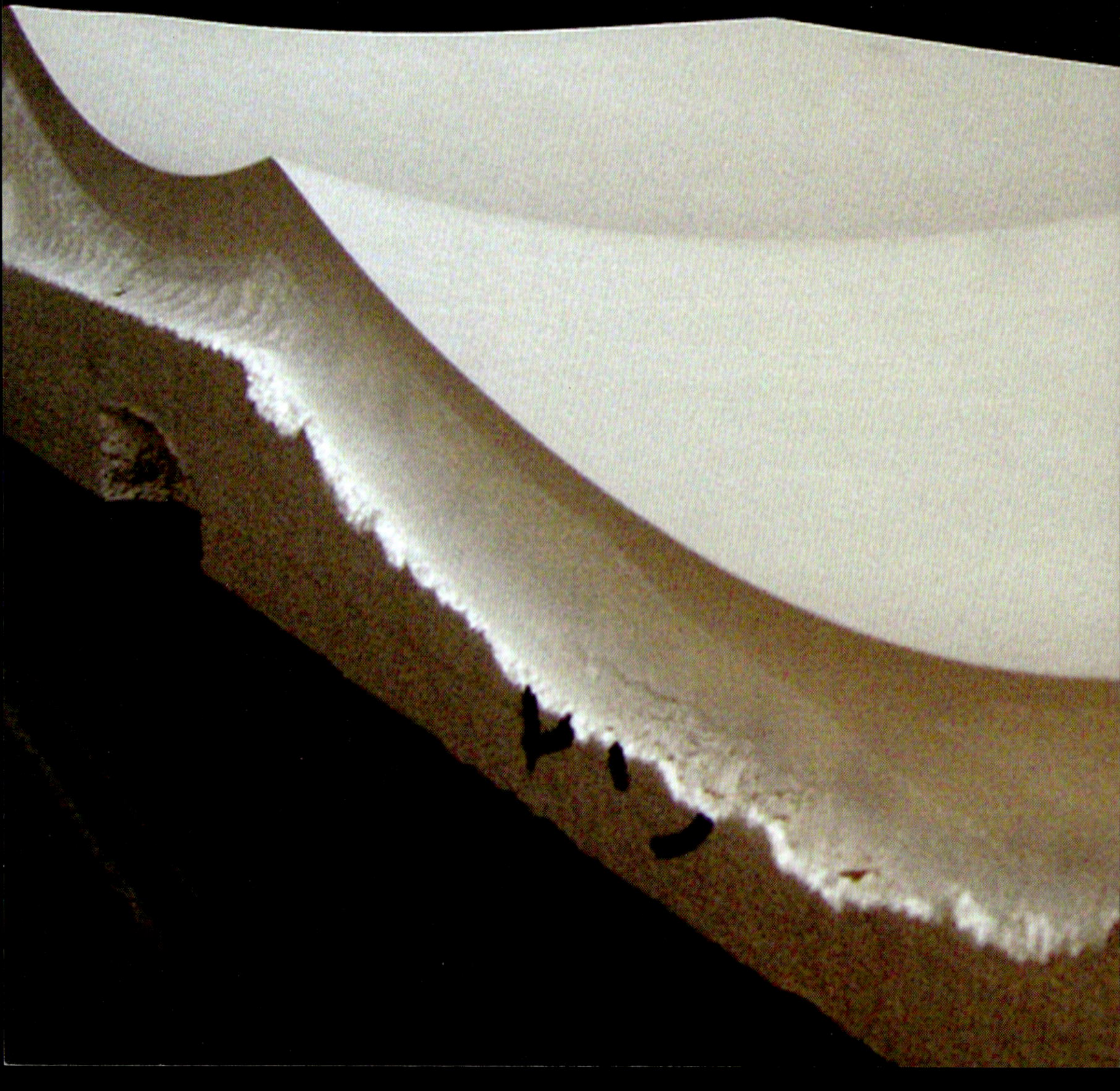

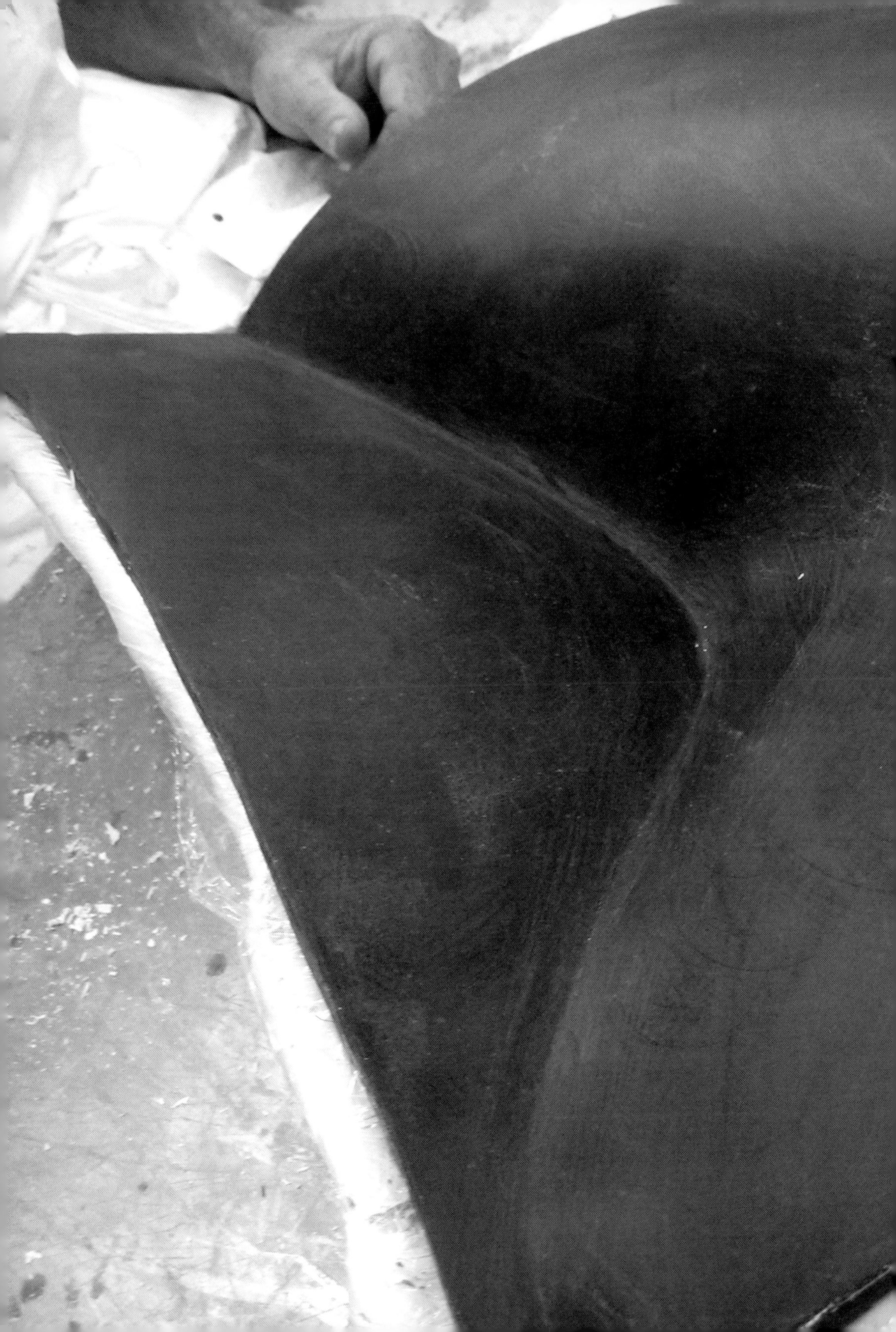

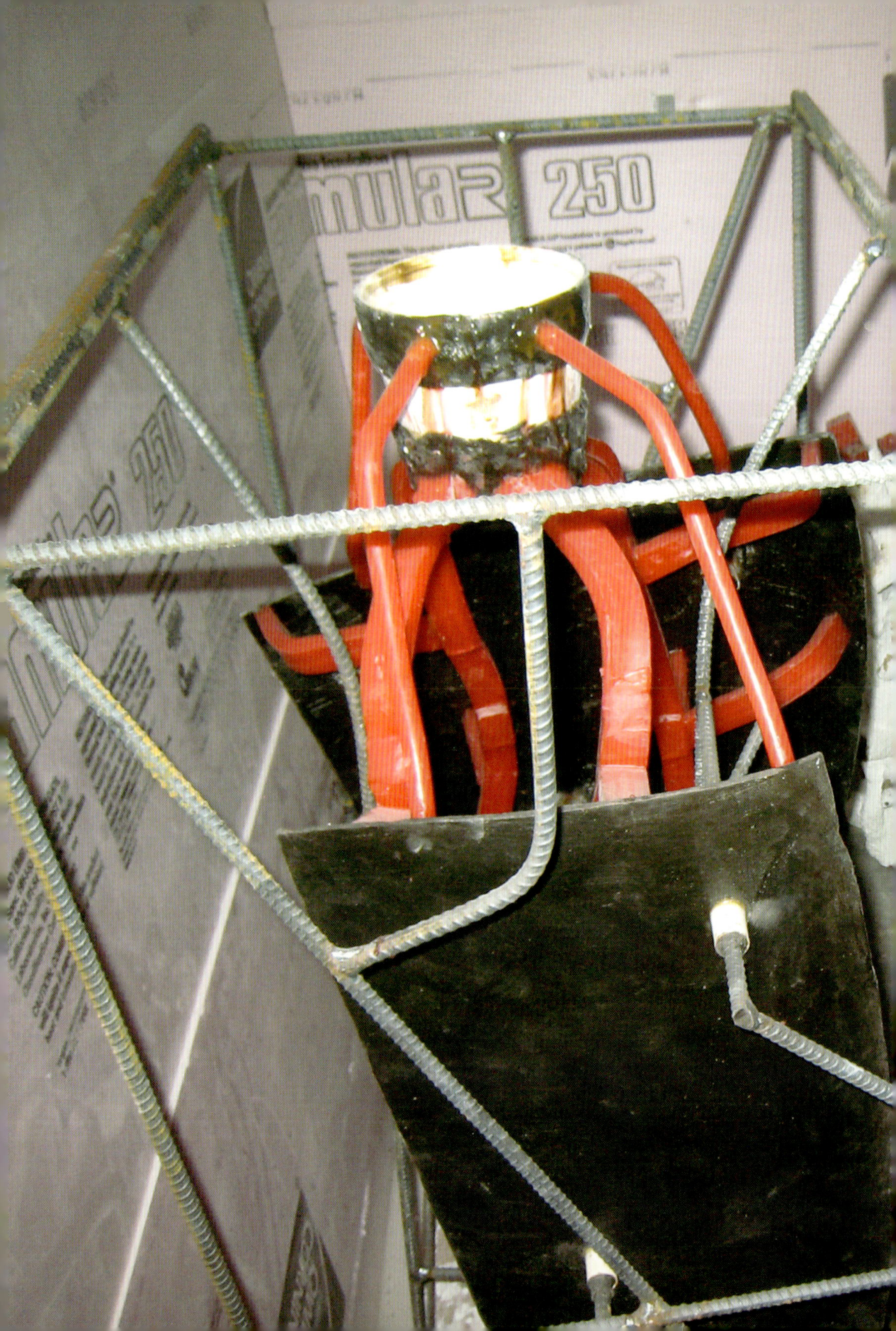
mular 250

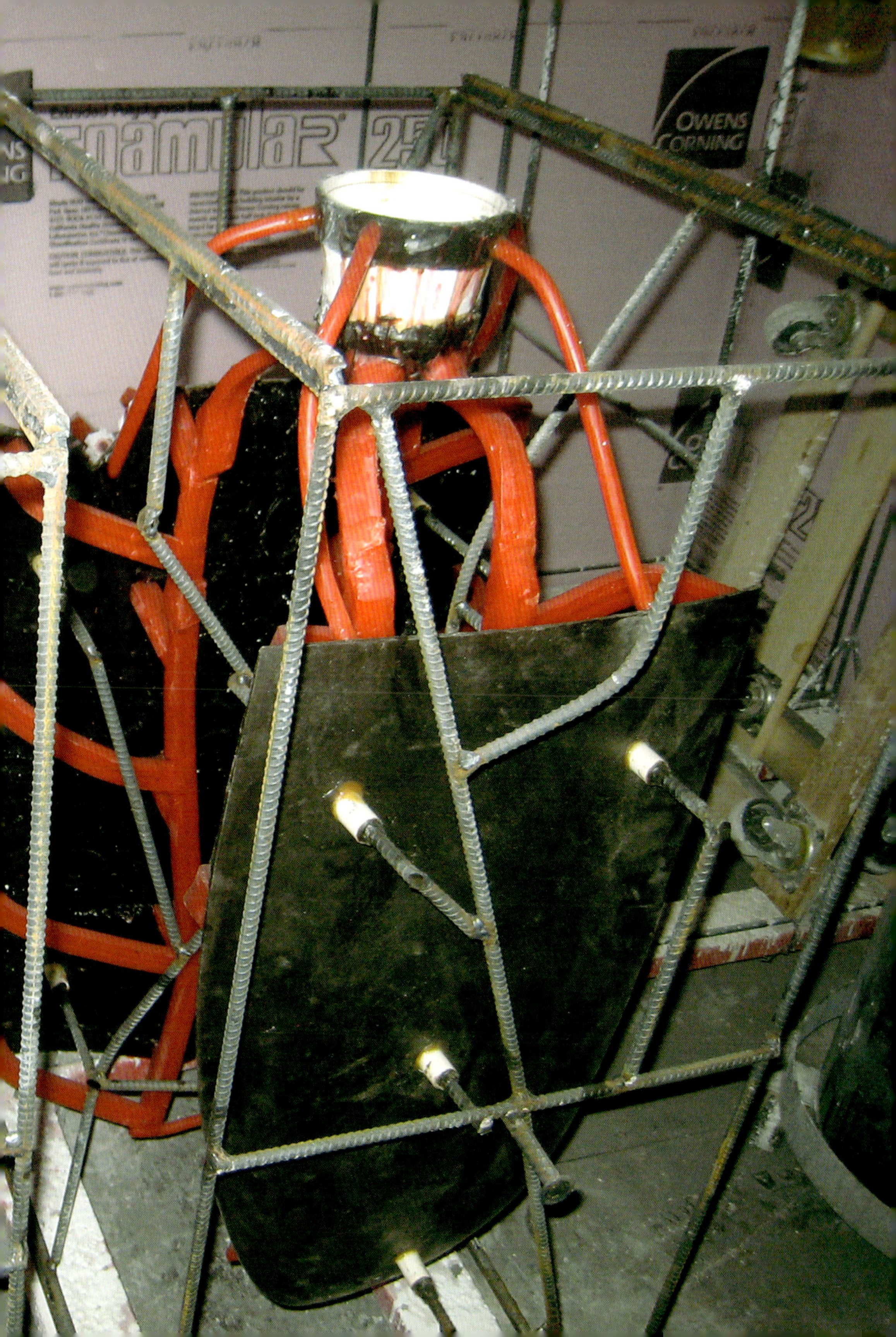
OWENS
CORNING

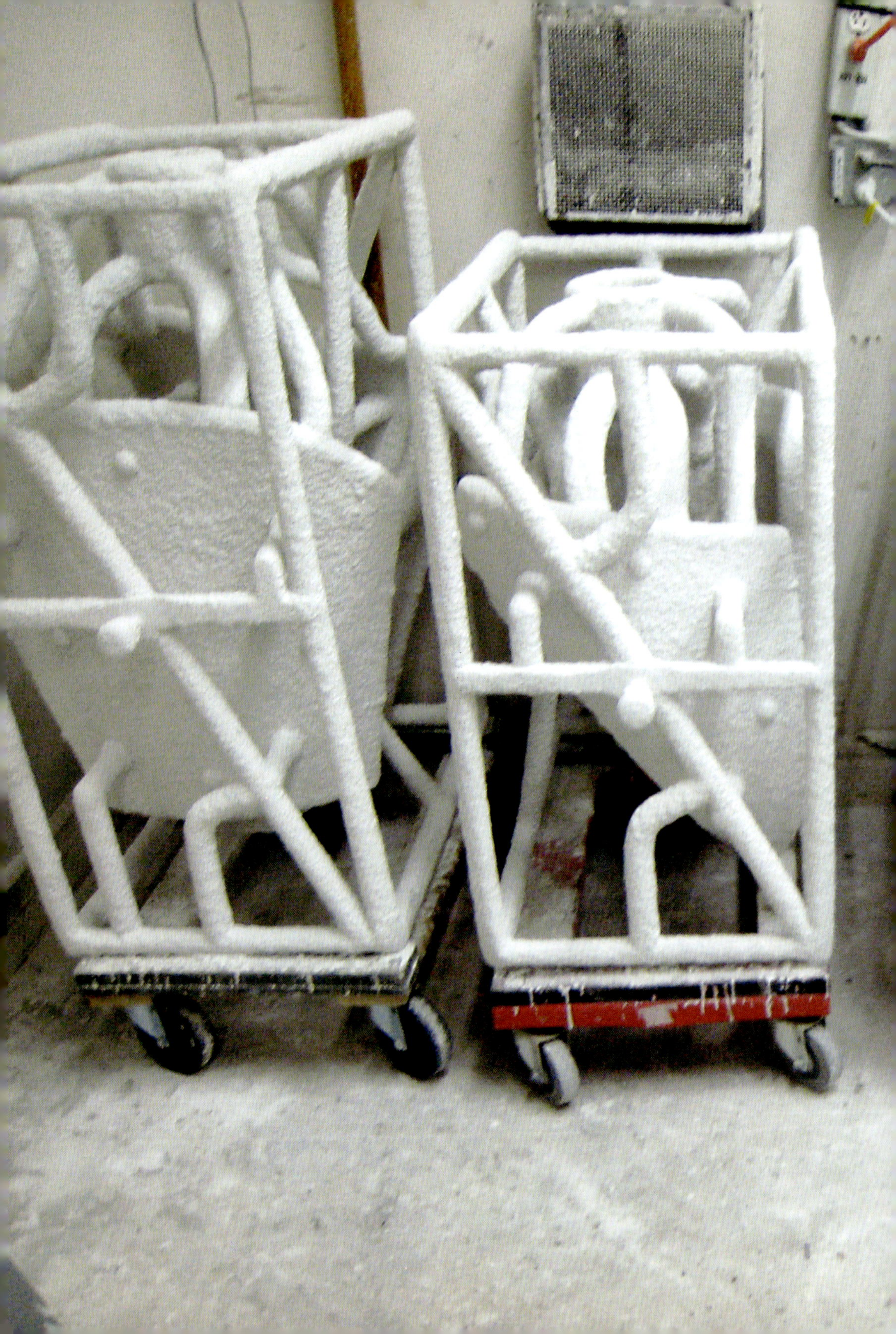

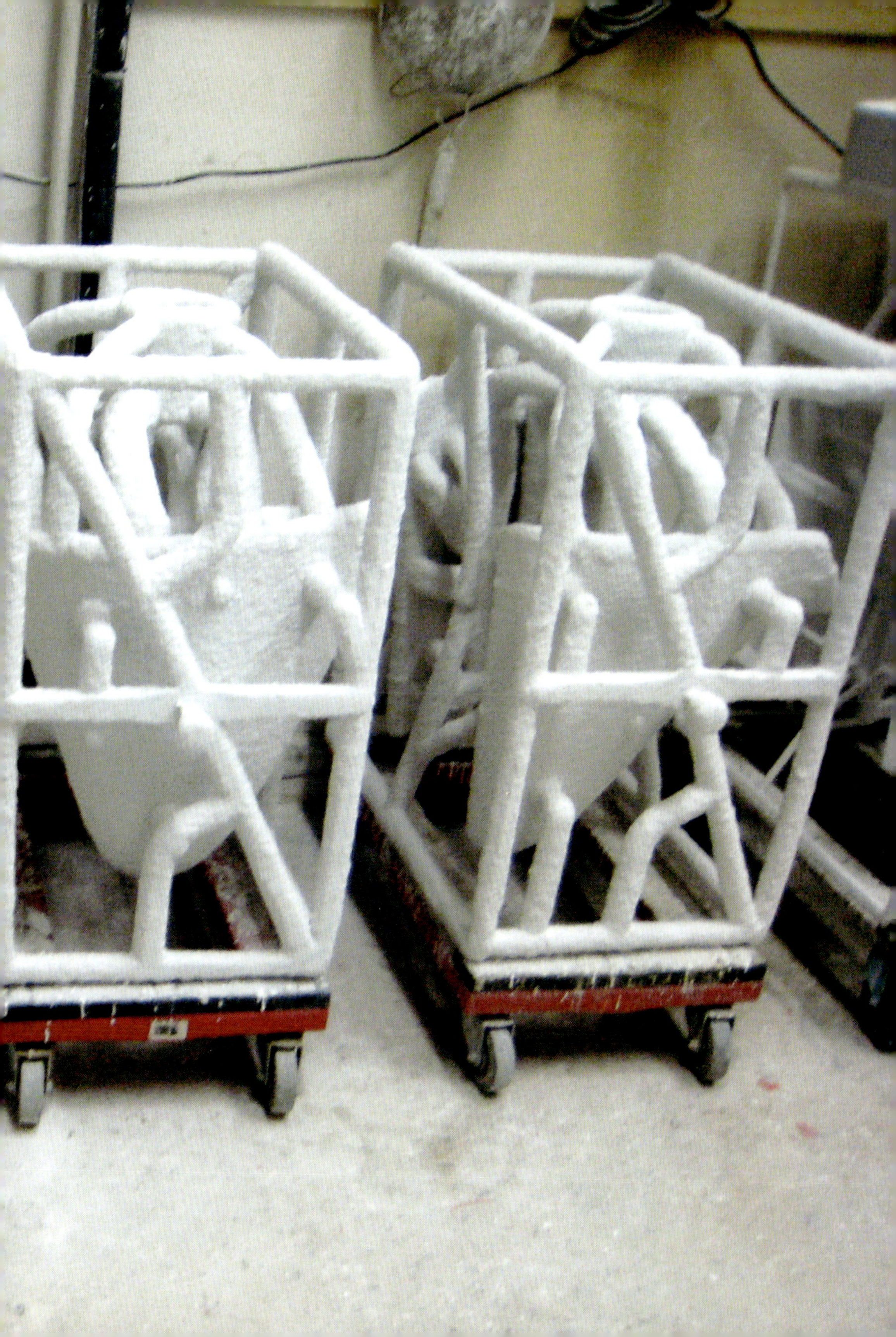

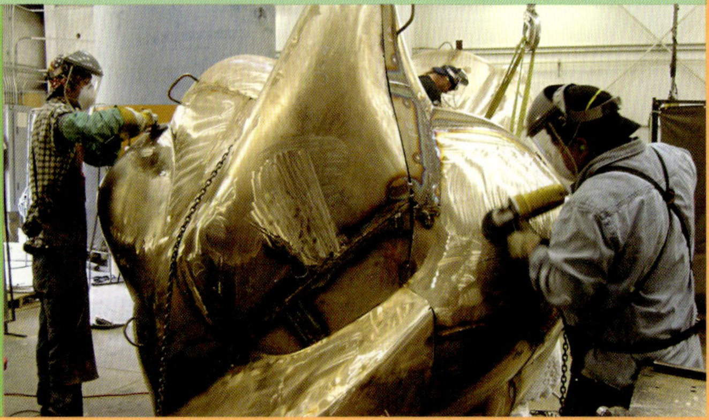

FABRICATION

The wax used at the Walla Walla foundry is a combination of M. Argueso Optimus and 2R738 recycled Wax. The melting temperature of the wax is 150 degrees and the wax is cast at a temperature of 200 degrees.

The Ceramic Shell is flash-fired at a temperature of 1650 degrees for two hours.

The Walla Walla foundry can pour a maximum of 1100 lbs of silicon bronze at one time. The thickness of the castings is 3/16 inch.

David Anderson

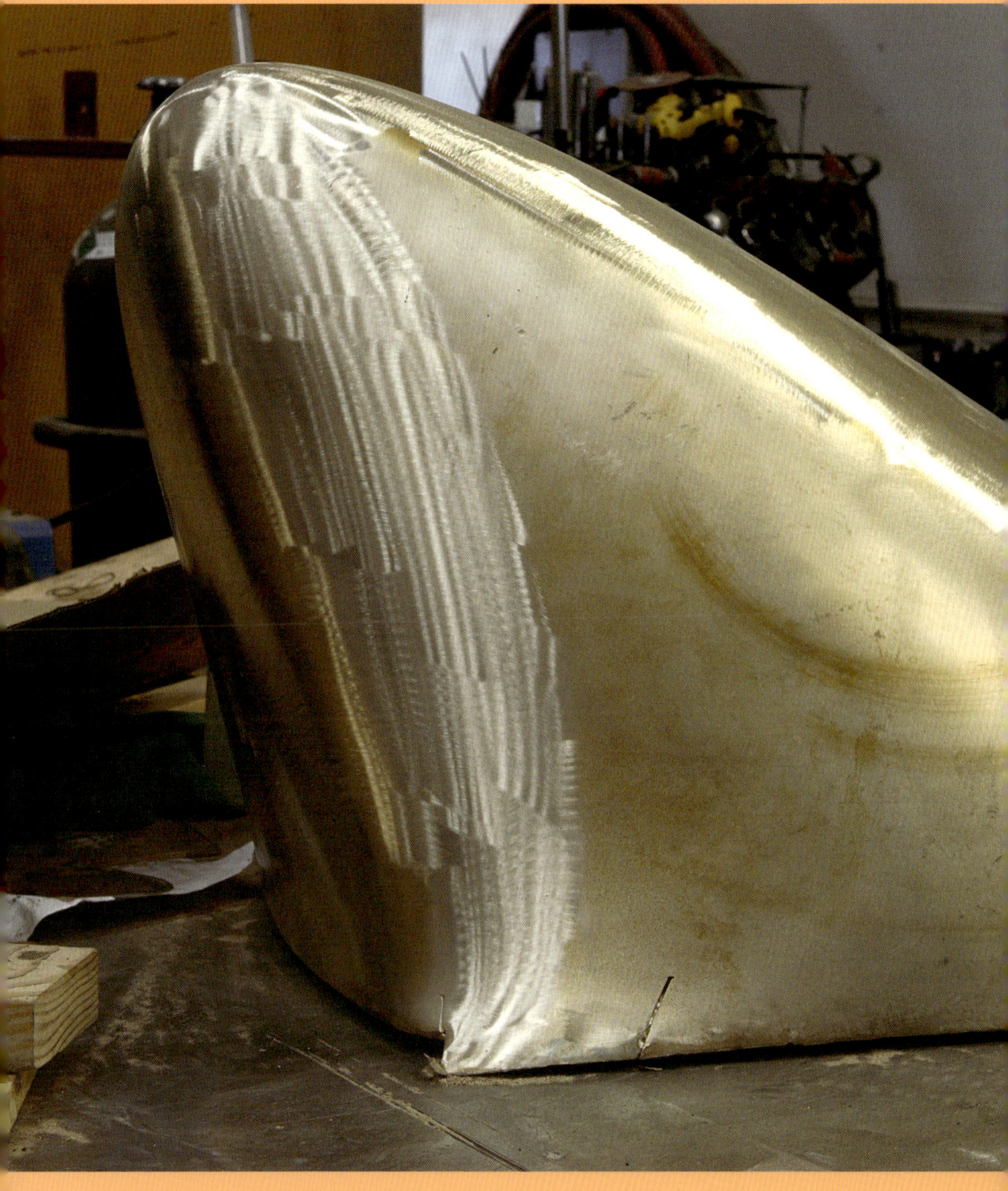

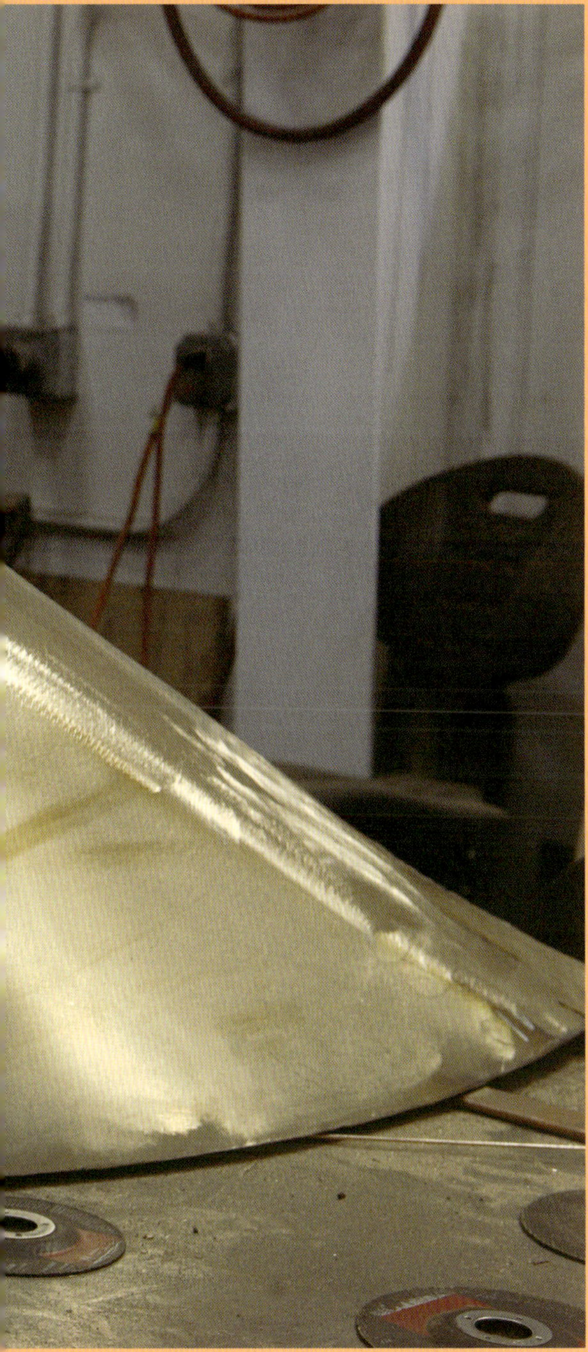

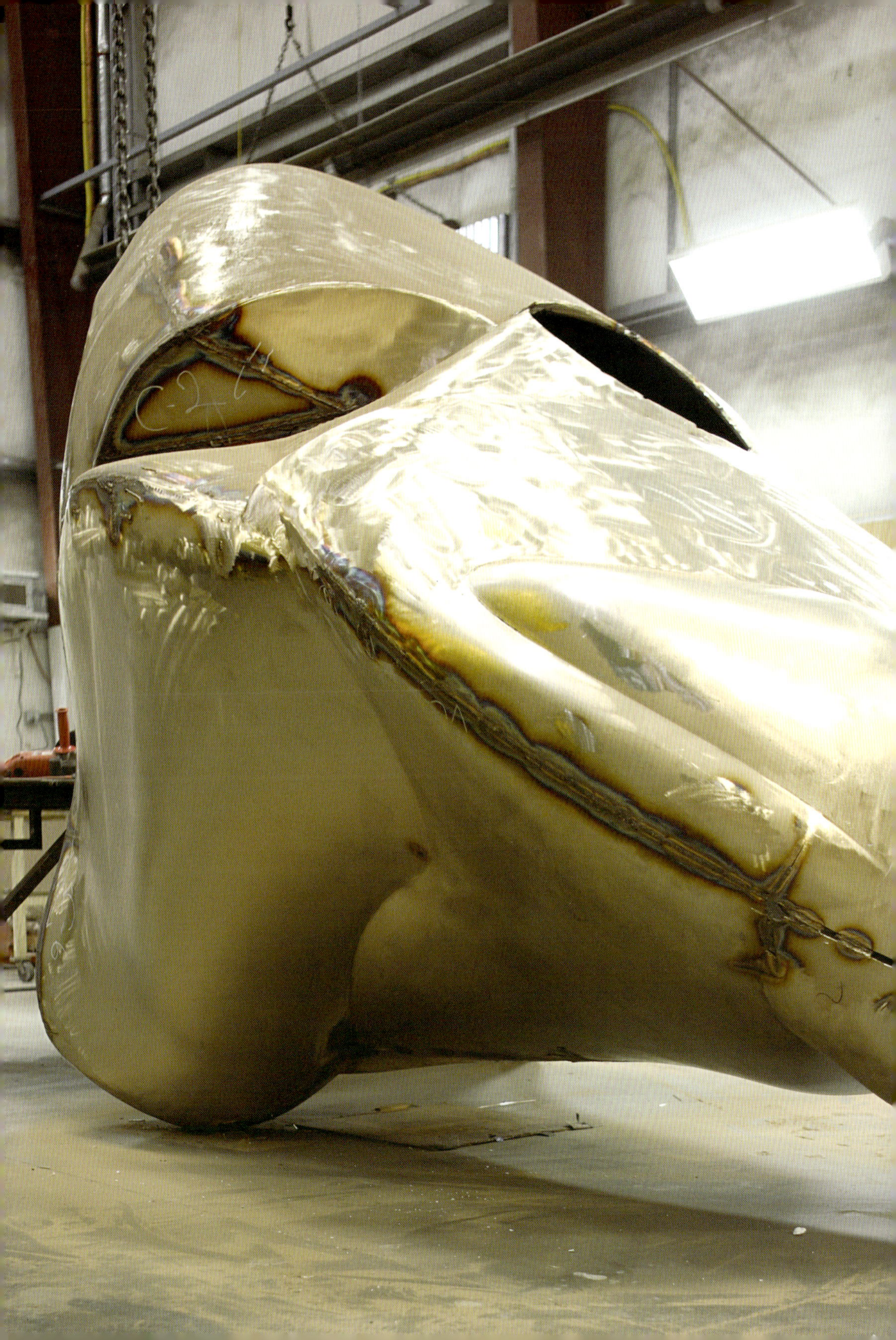

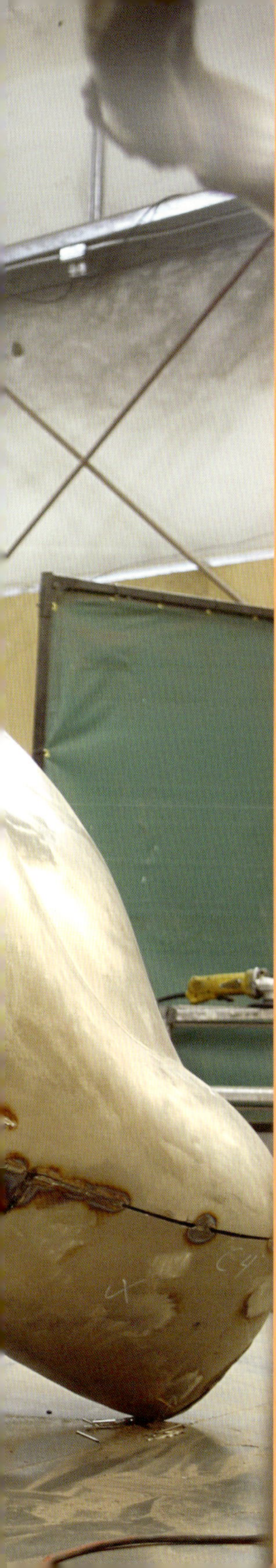

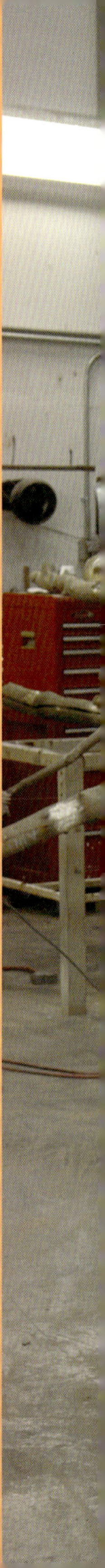

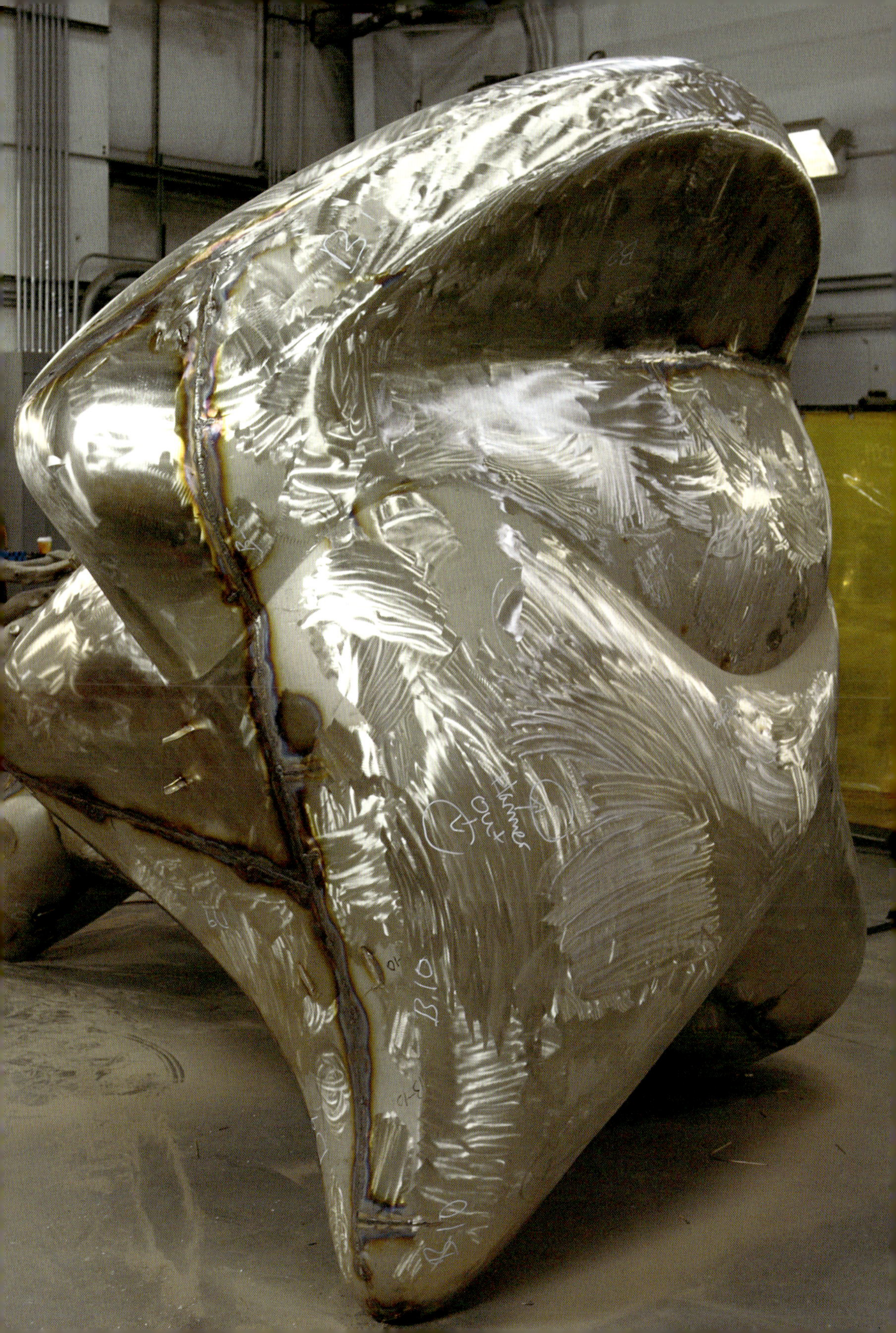

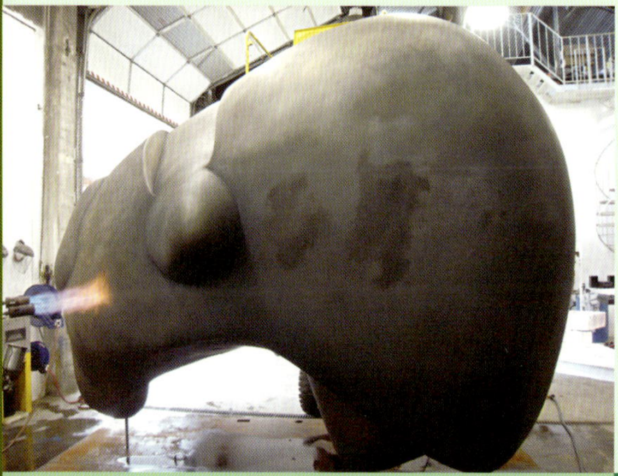

PATINATION

Chemicals:
Potash Sulfurated: 100g/gal
Ferric nitrate: 80 g/gal
Super black: Potash 6 parts to Ferric 1 part

Metal Prep:
Sandblasted

Patina Process:
Chemicals applied through an HVLP gun in a light mist on a heated surface

Finish:
Johnson's paste wax as directed by the conservator

Karl Longin

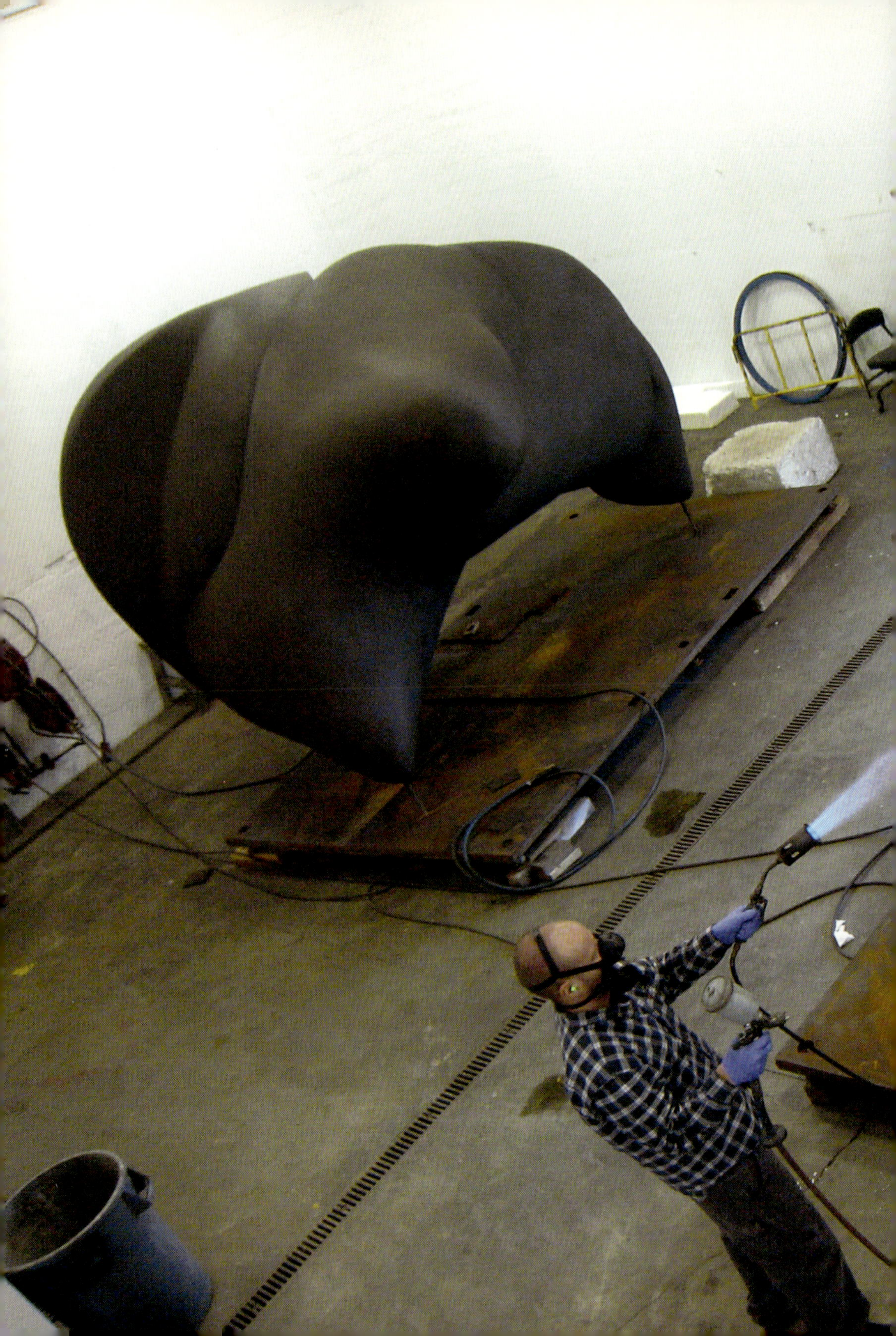

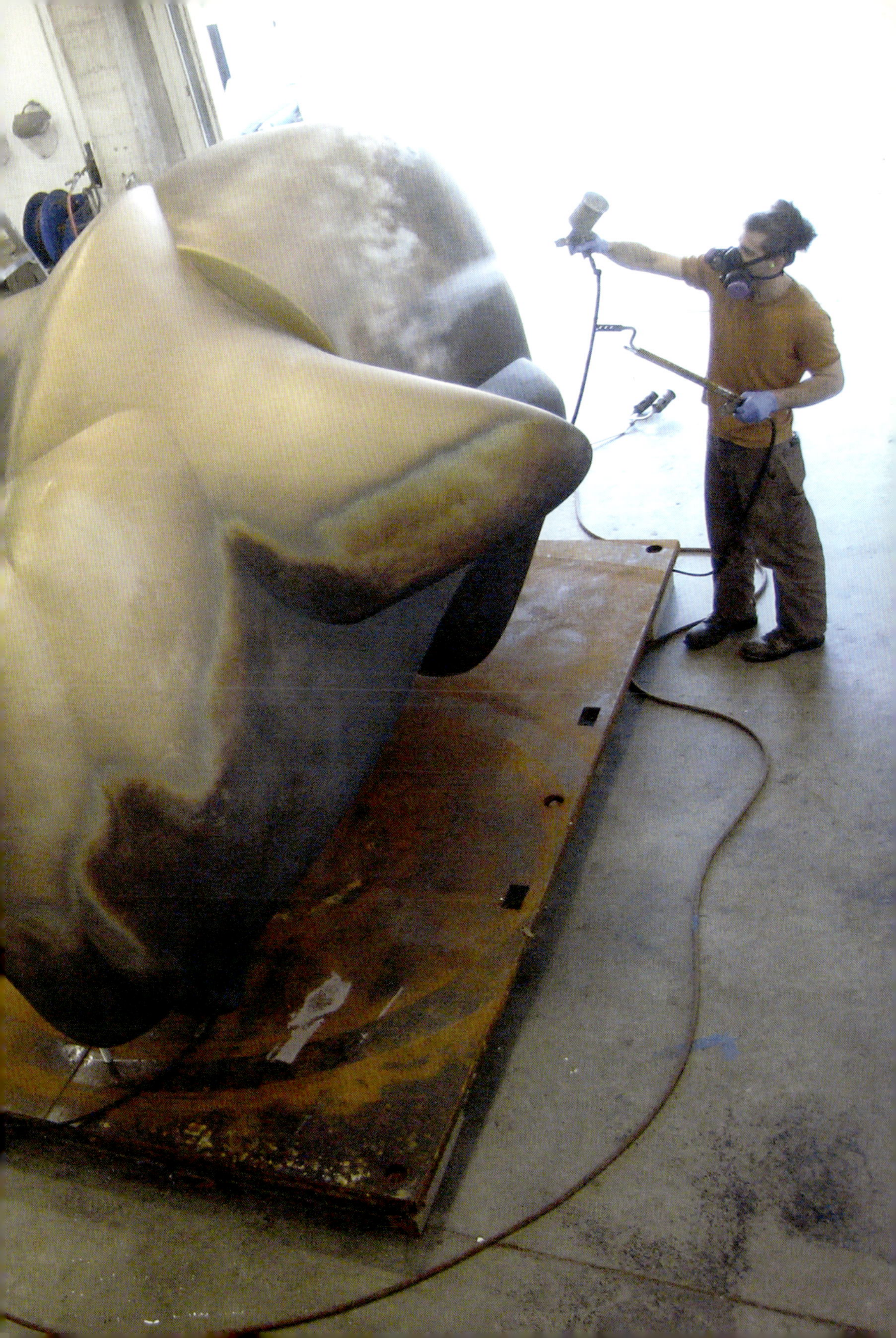

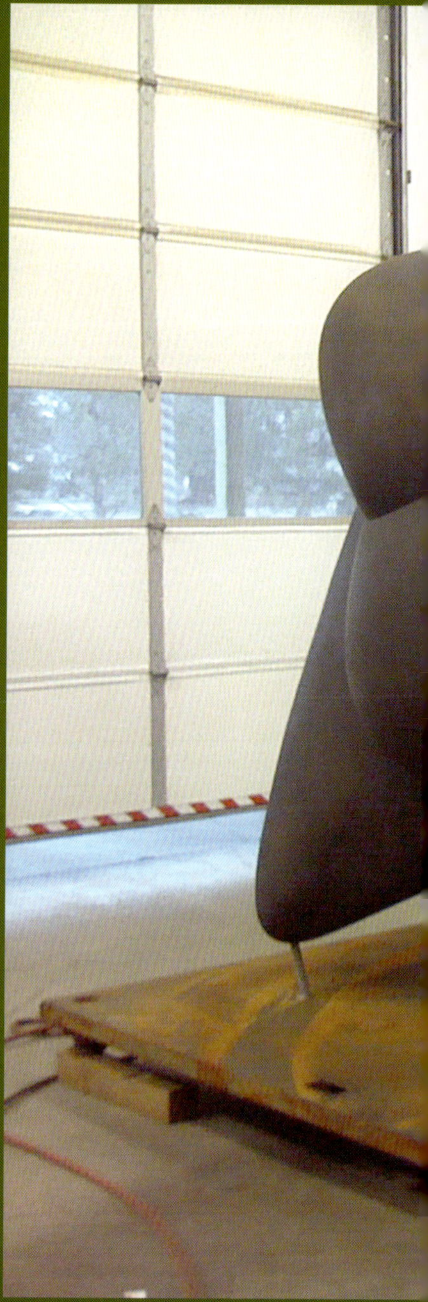

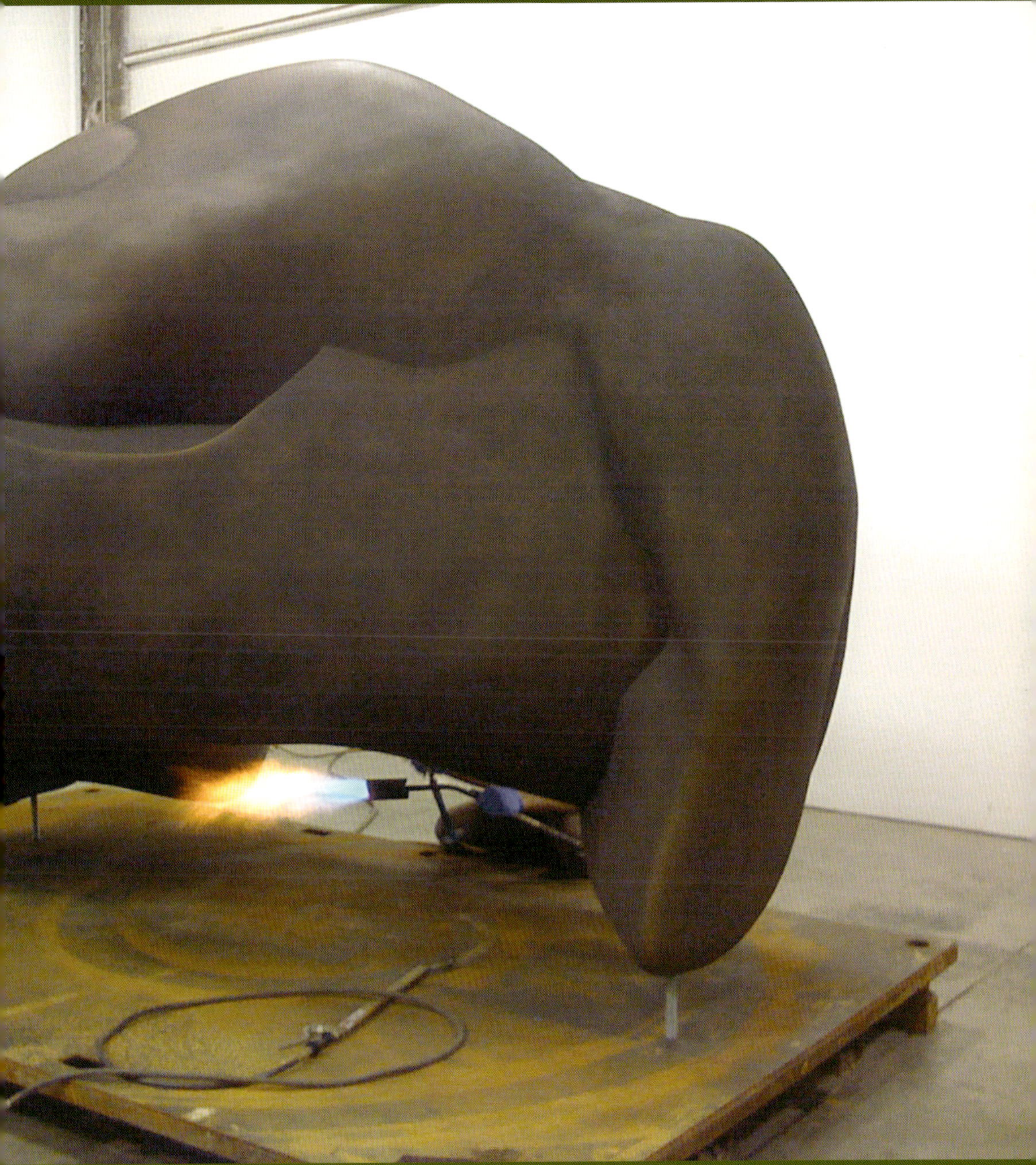

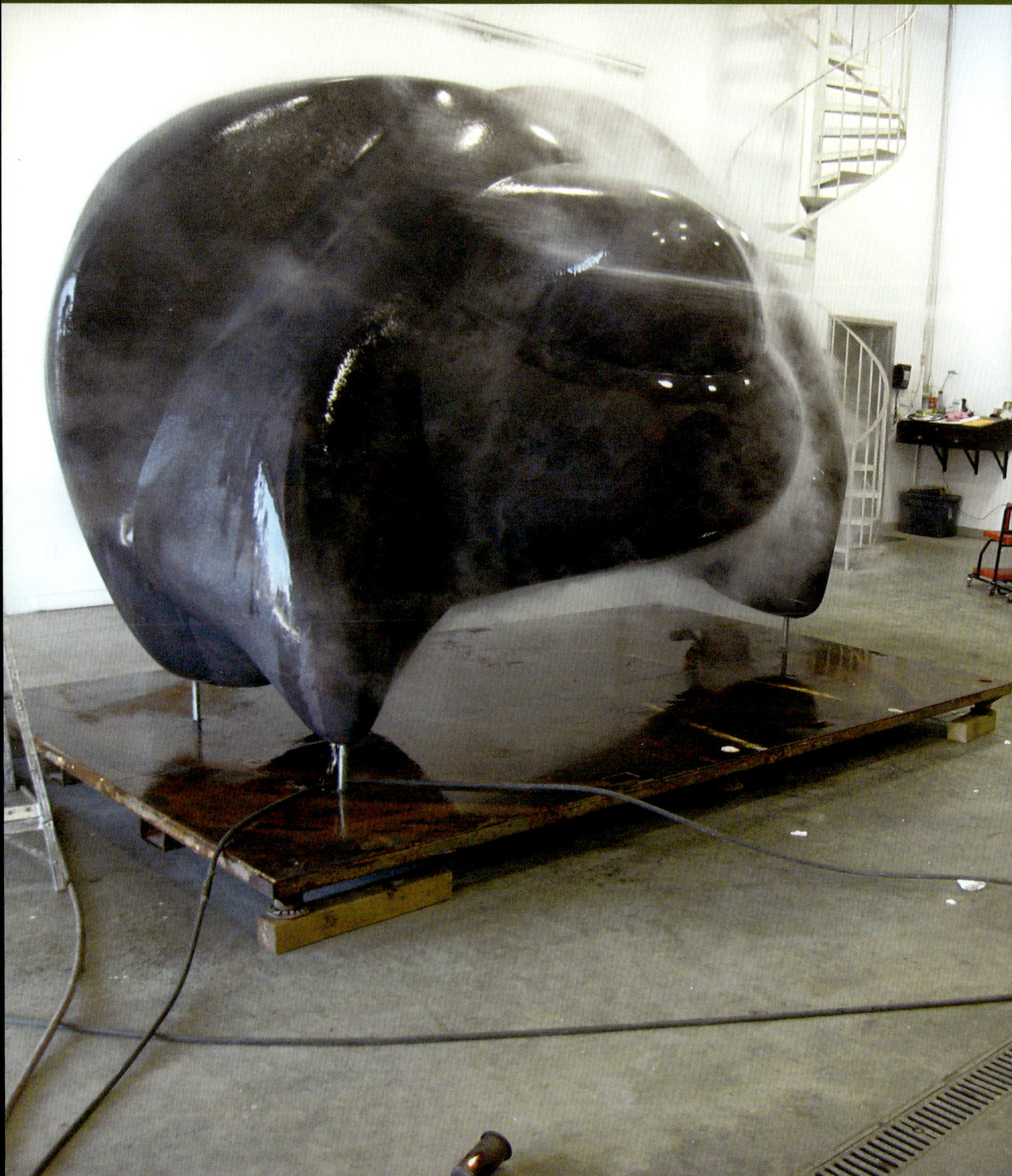

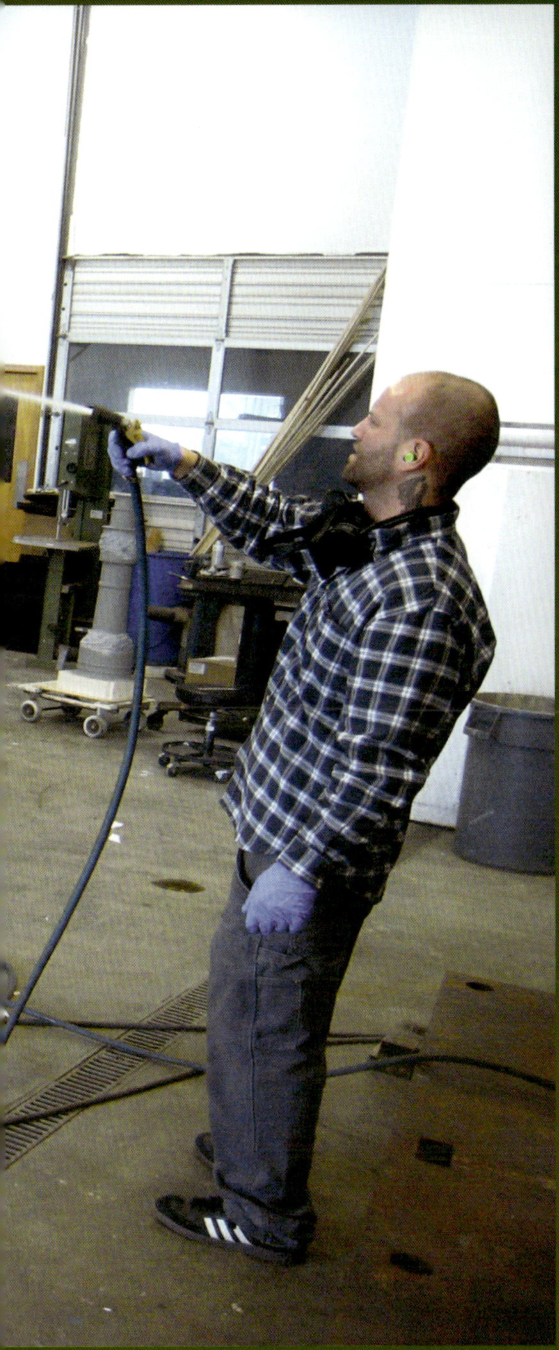

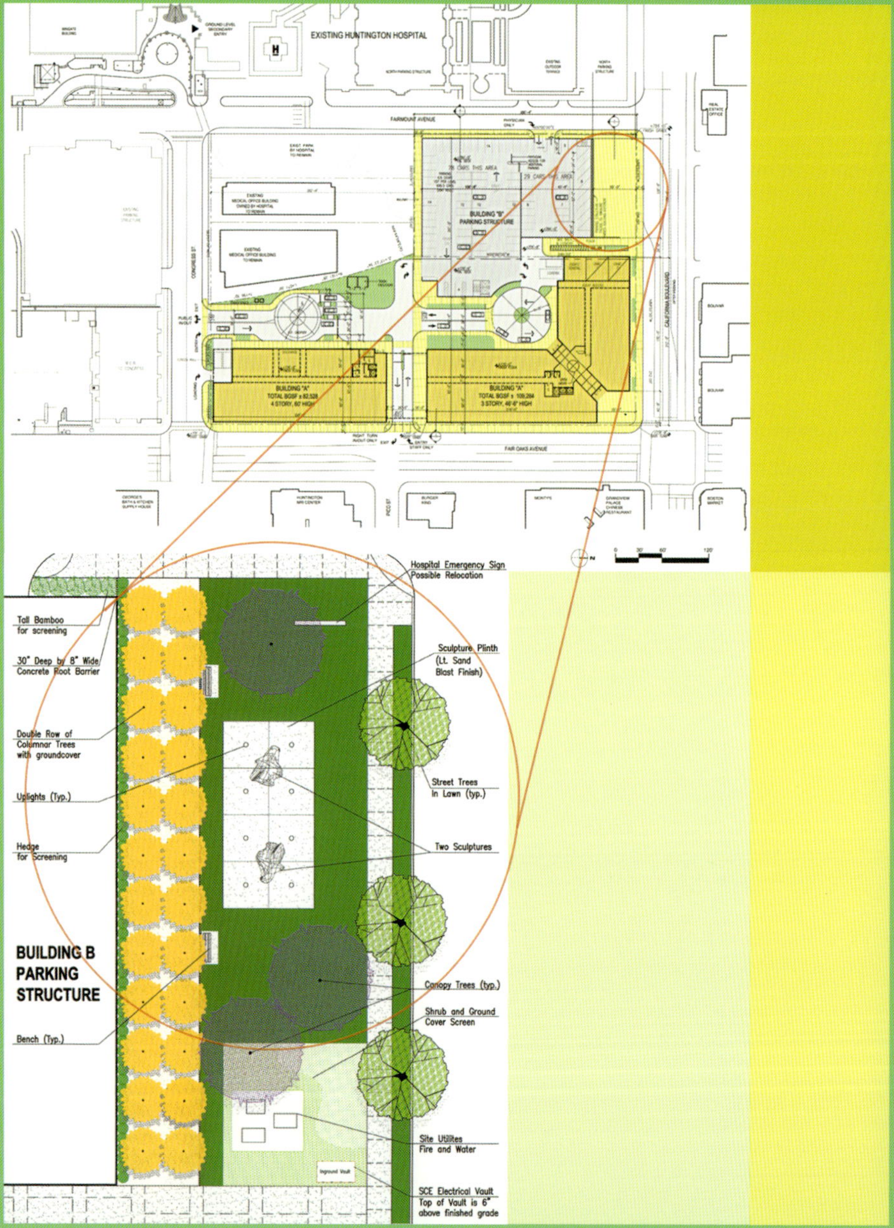
EXISTING HUNTINGTON HOSPITAL
FAIRMOUNT AVENUE
FAIR OAKS AVENUE
Hospital Emergency Sign
Possible Relocation
Tall Bamboo
for screening
30" Deep by 8" Wide
Concrete Root Barrier
Sculpture Plinth
(Lt. Sand
Blast Finish)
Double Row of
Columnar Trees
with groundcover
Street Trees
in Lawn (typ.)
Uplights (Typ.)
Two Sculptures
Hedge
for Screening
BUILDING B
PARKING
STRUCTURE
Canopy Trees (typ.)
Shrub and Ground
Cover Screen
Bench (Typ.)
Site Utilites
Fire and Water
SCE Electrical Vault
Top of Vault is 6"
above finished grade

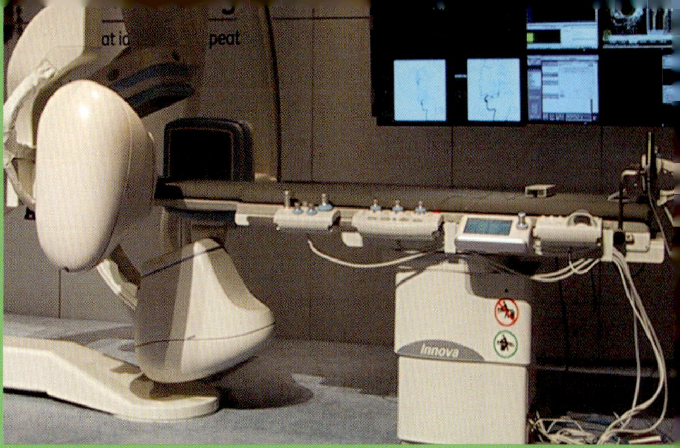

OUTPATIENT PAVILION

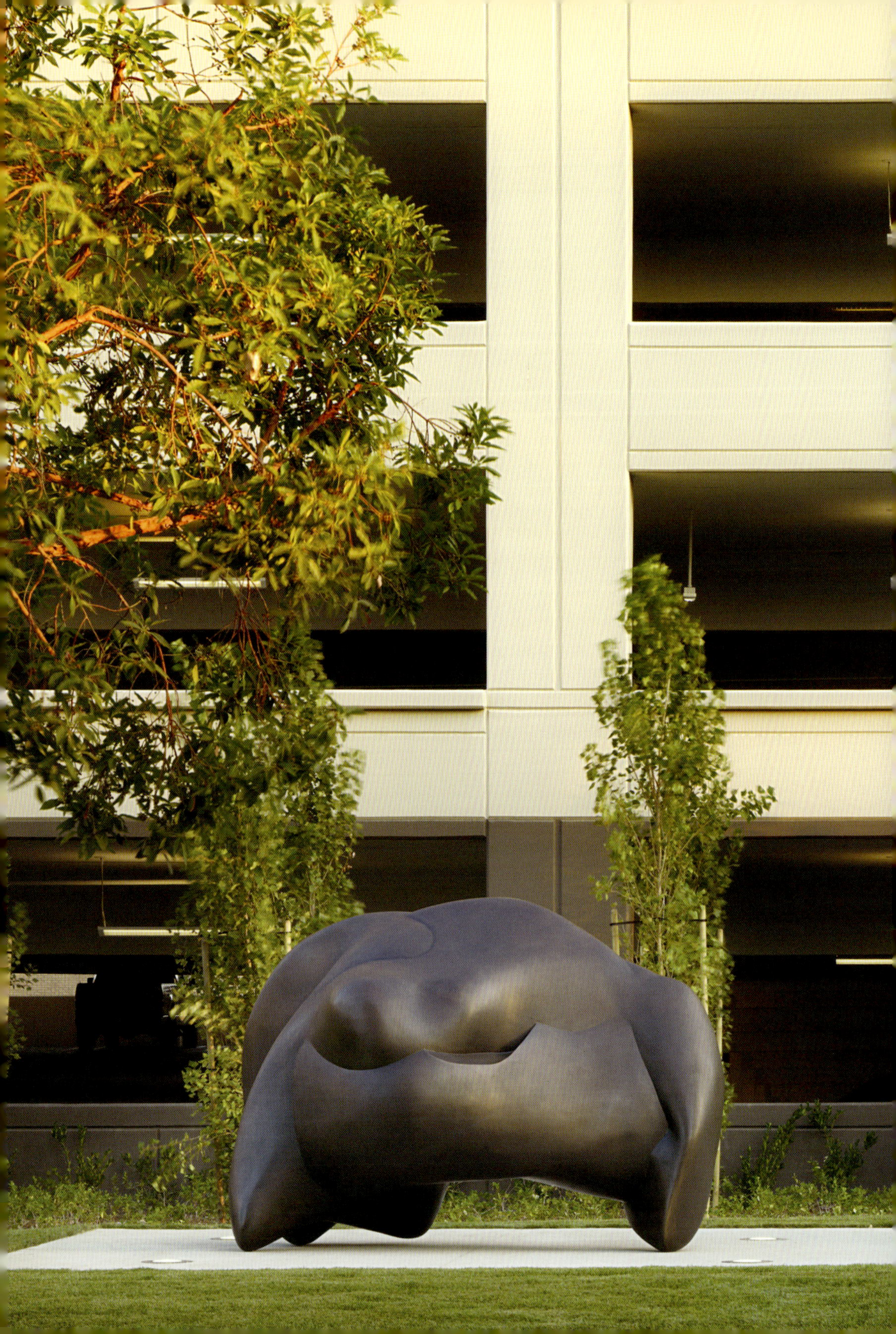

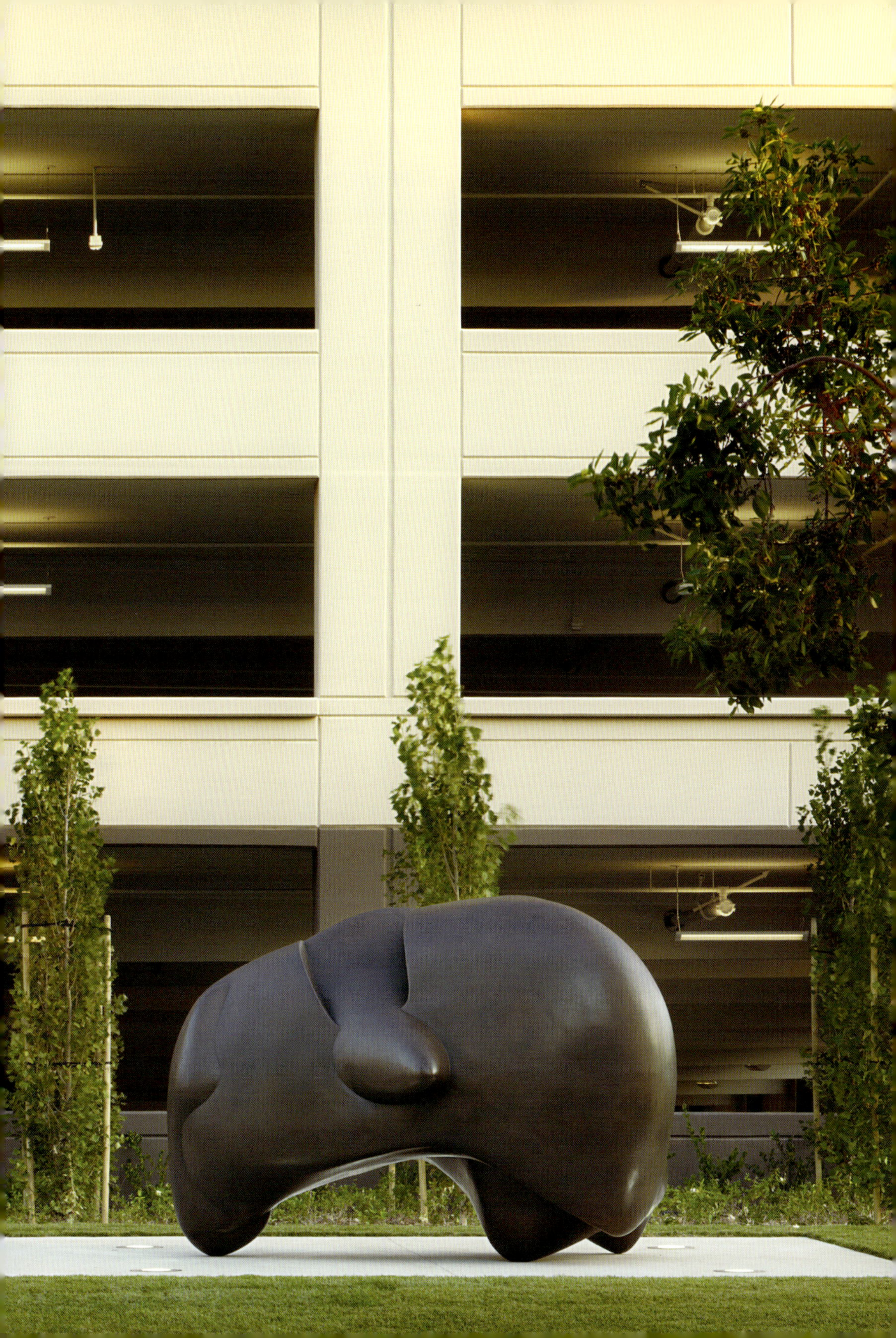

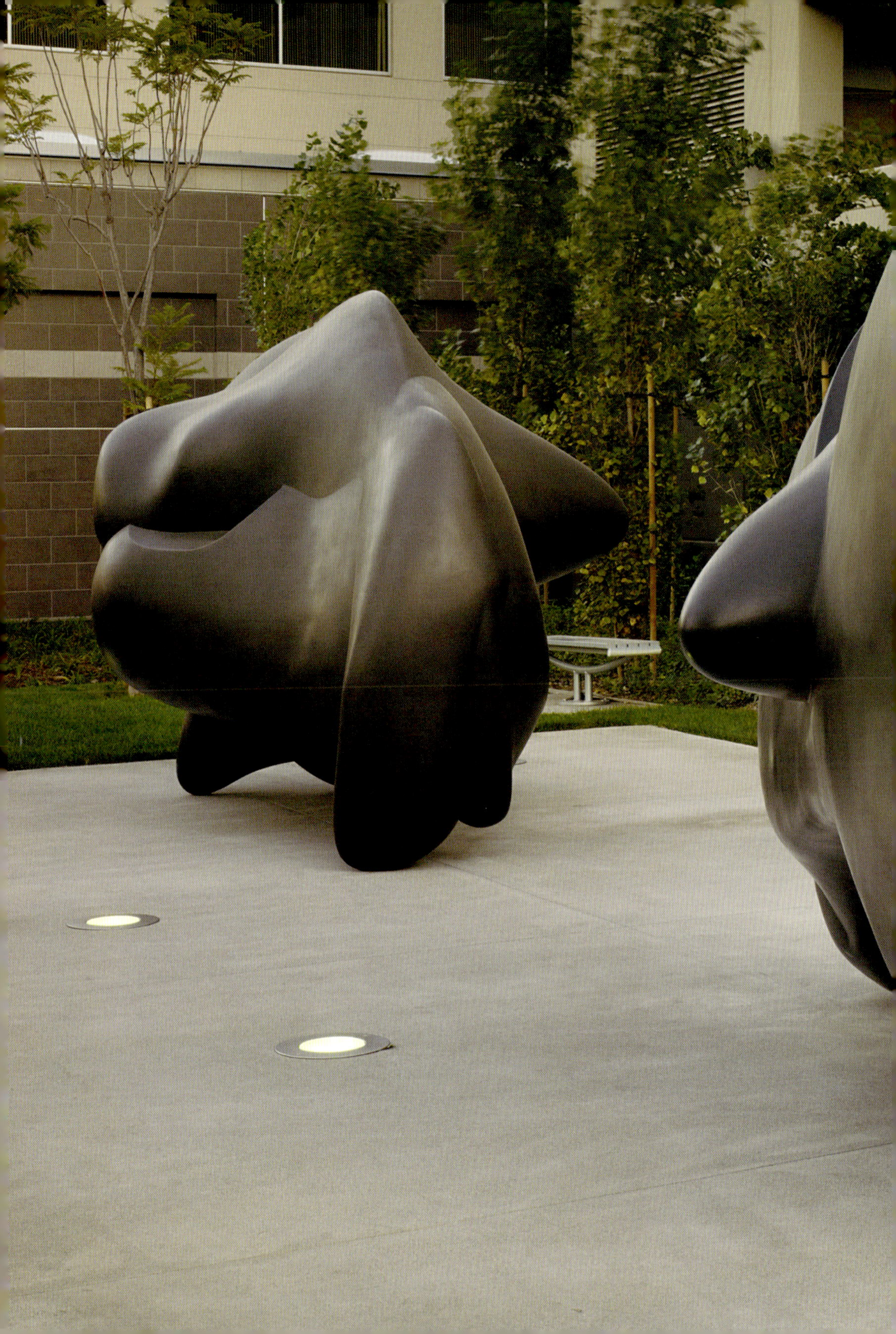

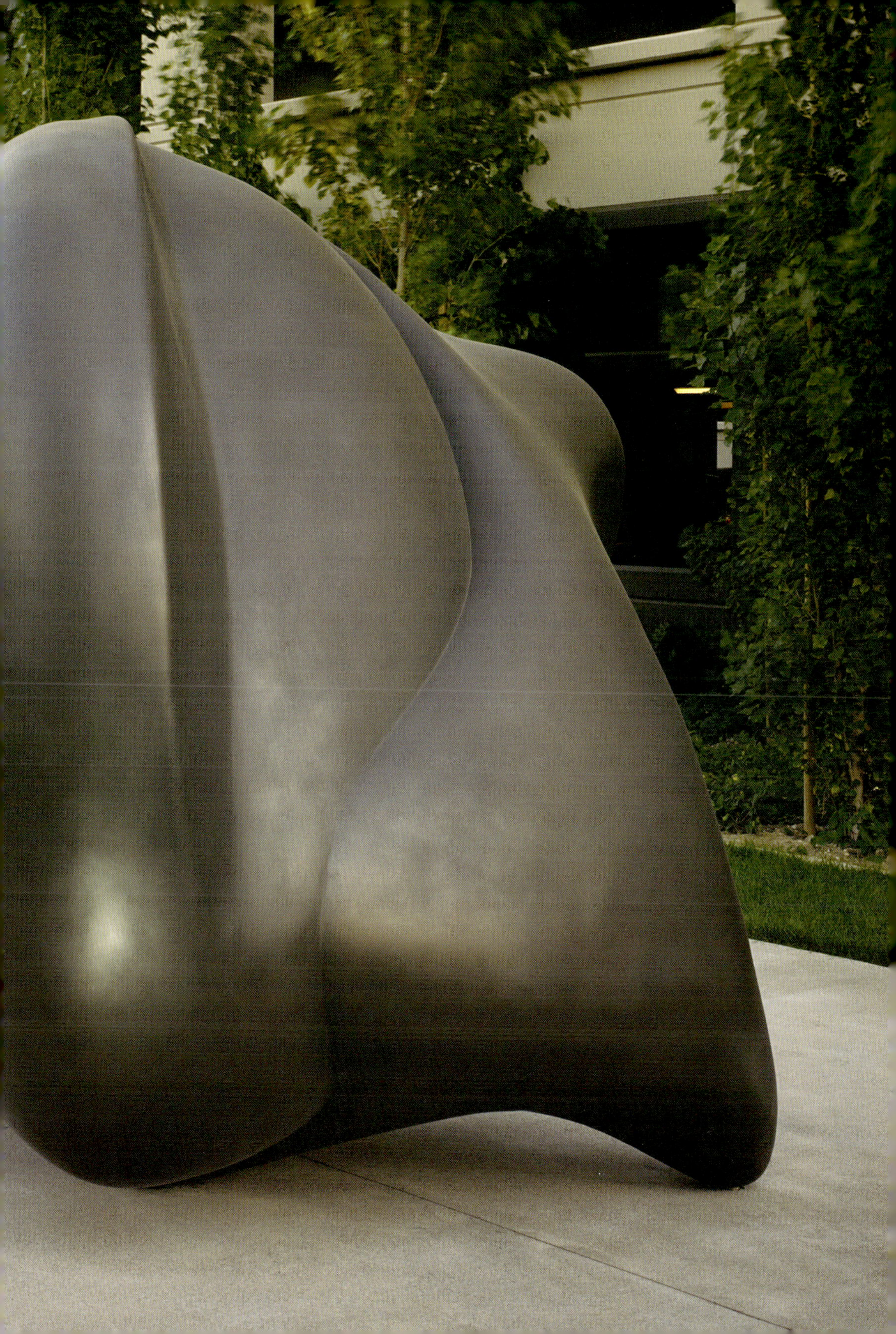

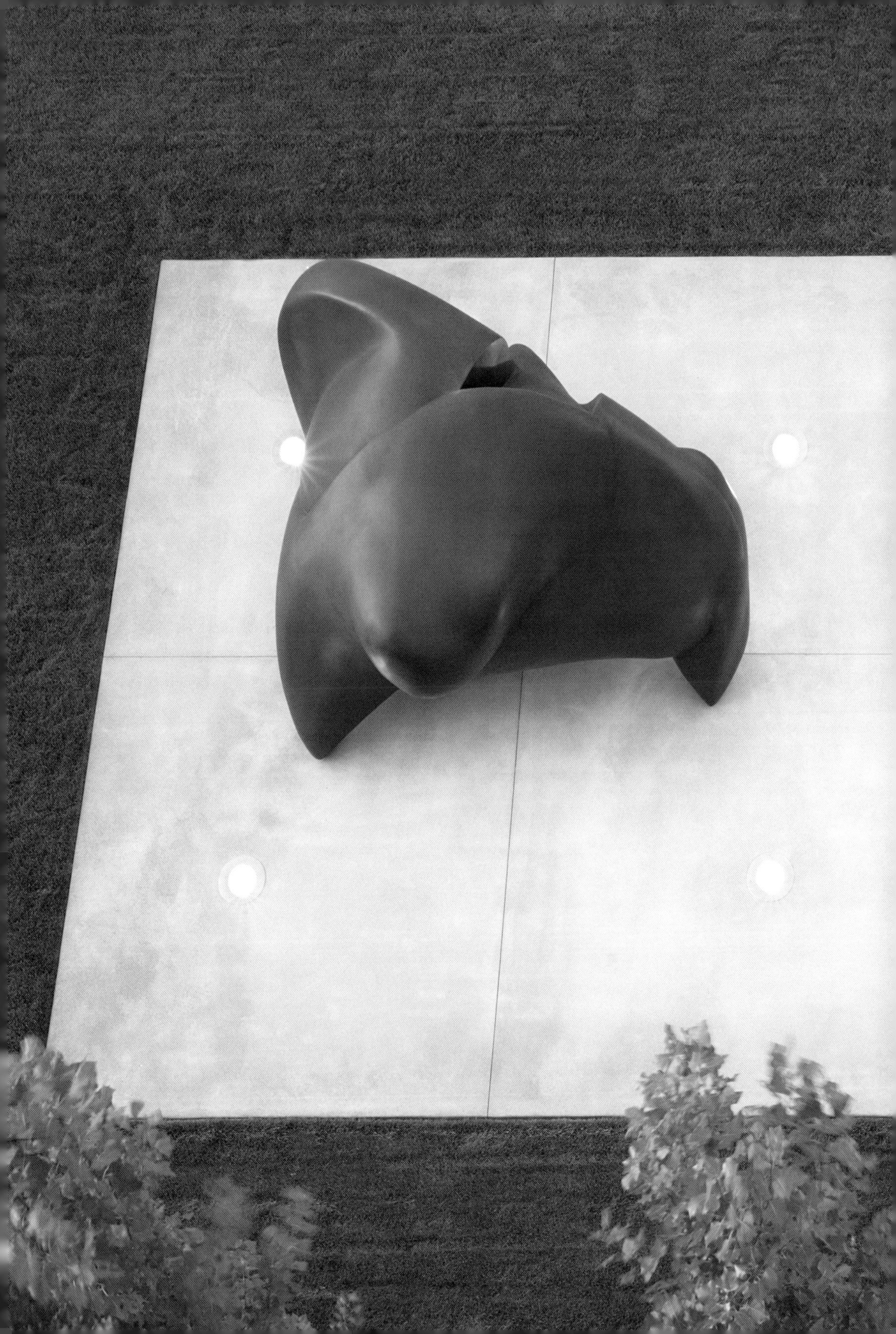

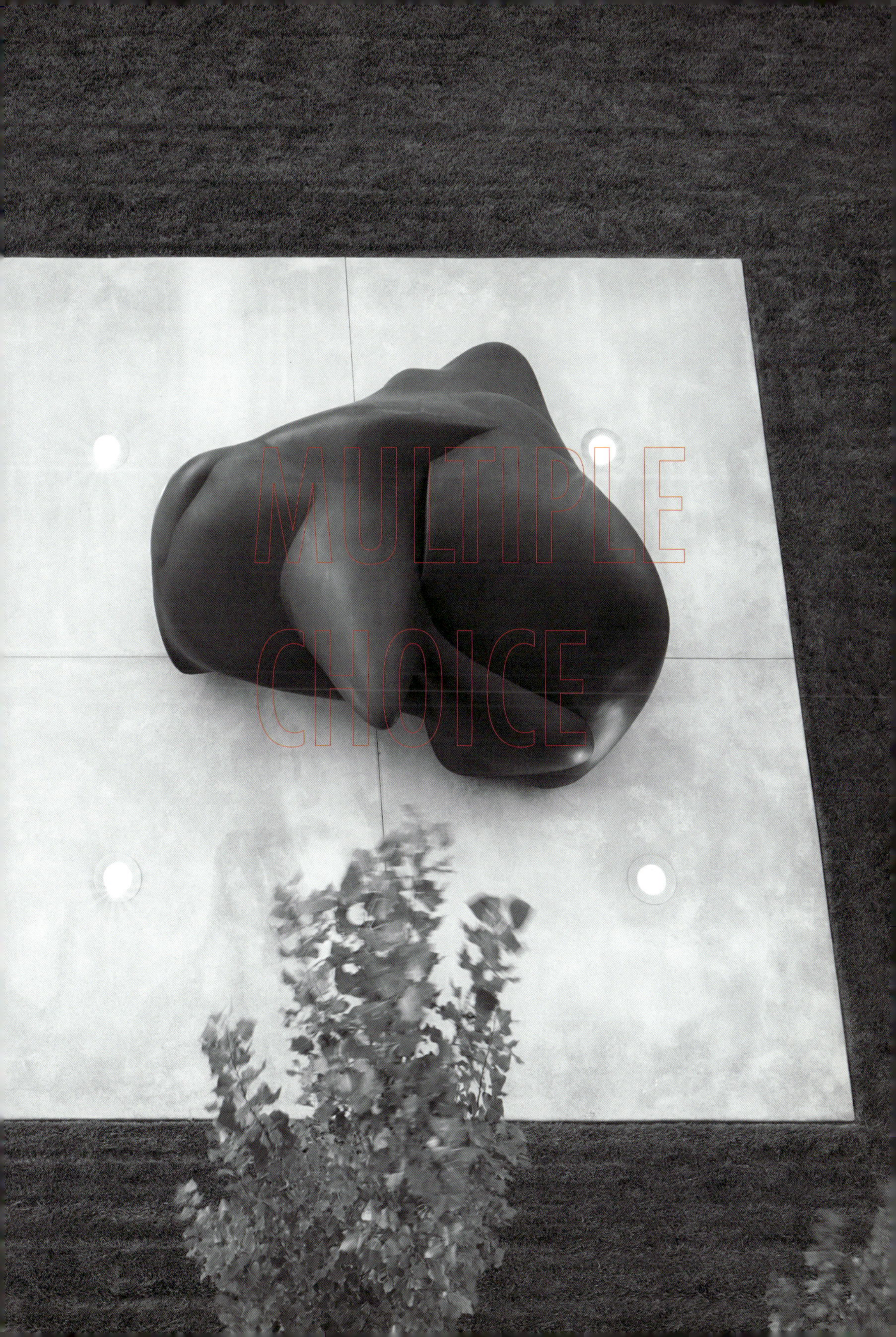

MULTIPLE CHOICE

Multiple Choice: On *Separated United Forms* by David Schafer

Jan Tumlir

What Is It?

Perhaps, it goes without saying—and yet I'll say it: writing about art is not literature because it has an object that exists. It has an object that is not strictly imaginary, as are the objects of novels and stories, but then again, it is also not strictly concrete either. This is because, first, the object of art writing, like that of any other writing, is not *there*. The art object is absent to the writing; all that lies within the reach of the author and reader alike is "writing (storing) writing—no more, no less,"[1] as Friedrich Kittler puts it. Second, the object of art writing, unlike that of most other writing, is one to which we do tend to grant an imaginary status.

Why mention any of this now, again? Because David Schafer is an artist who reads a great deal of writing about art—as well as that about architecture, design, music, and many more things besides—and often responds to it in his work. It is characteristic of his practice that the written response to art is in turn responded to artistically, which is not to suggest that Schafer makes art about writing about art (or that he makes what is disparagingly termed "theory-driven art"); rather, he acknowledges the dialogical element implicit within it. Moreover, one could say that inasmuch as his work stands its ground on this point, it proclaims the dialogical element as implicit in all works.

Once we can no longer consider the work of art as a wholly-made imaginary thing, it confronts us instead as a complex sedimentation of worldly givens and ideational variables, each of which is comprised as much of word-things as thing-words. This analytical description of the creative work is very much the product of a certain moment in art education that Schafer and I have shared, and it is modeled on a selection of theoretical texts that continue to reverberate in our thoughts—notably, Roland Barthes's "From Work to Text" and Michel Foucault's "What Is an Author?"[2] These no longer provide the core principles of the art school curriculum, and it is for this reason that I want to recall them here. The 1980s, our "formative period," is now itself often written off as "theory-driven," but it would be more accurate to say that it was a time when art and writing had managed to define a point of common interest in the analytical object. At any rate, it is precisely this "kind" of object that takes shape at the intersection between Schafer's practice and this essay.

What is it? The analytical object must first be distinguished from the real and existing object that one confronts in person, "out there" in the world. Whether organic or artificial, constructed from scratch or found already made, the real and existing object is characterized by its integrity, a being-for-itself that corresponds to its apartness from us. In contrast, the analytical object is one already undergoing the process of intellectual appropriation, which also always entails some degree of decomposition. From thing to idea to word and so on, the real and existing object is broken down into parts as it is analyzed. Simple enough when considered from the perspective of one who writes about art—as even the most anodyne forms of "objective" description constitute an assault on the integrity of their object—the analytical object is somewhat more difficult to imagine from the perspective of the artist. To merely reverse the course of the breakdown would be to tell only half of the story, since Schafer's work is not only made out of words, but also the things that they relate to, in whole and in part. Moreover, the objective outcome of this making does not confront us with its integrity restored. Comprised of broken-up parts, it will remain to the end a pieced-together thing.

All artists furnish us with potentially analytical objects inasmuch as any work can be analyzed. Some artists insist on analysis, whereas others evade it; Schafer does both—which is also to say, neither. As pieced-together things, his works have already processed their breakdown, rendering any further analysis somewhat redundant. If Sigmund Freud has very little to say about cinema, for example, this is because it not only anticipates his questions, but enacts them in its form. Much the same holds true for the work "at hand," which—like all of Schafer's work, only perhaps more so—does not readily cede to analysis, assuming instead a more proactive, authorial role in the process.

The imaginary line that connects the art object to the subjectivity of the artist has already been cut. Schafer's work is scrupulously emptied of any interiority that one might want to ascribe to him alone. There is no individual source from which everything that

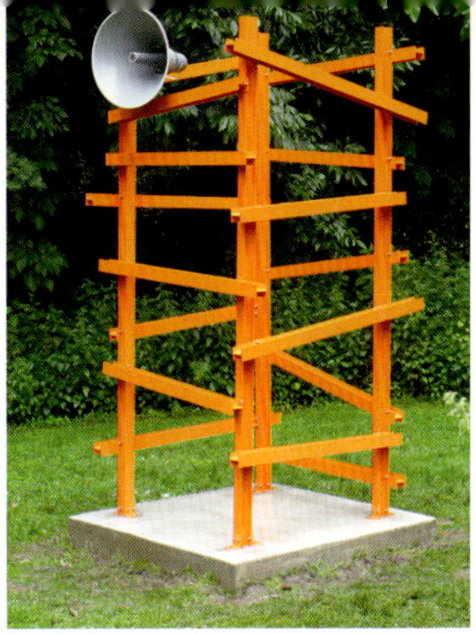

"Untitled Expression: How to Look at Sculpture," 2009, Abington Art Center, Philadelphia, Pennsylvania

comprises the work—all the various parts that could be extracted from it under analysis—is seen to emanate. But there is a point at which they converge, and that is right where you and I are.

A. I Don't Know...

In order to analyze an analytical object, one must undergo a process of self-analysis. Such an object prompts this approach by at first begging the questions that are put to it, only to turn them back out, one after another, onto its audience. In this way, it makes explicit the fact that one cannot really know anything outside oneself; whatever is known has been taken in, consumed, and digested, and is thereby no longer what it originally was. By way of its breakdown, the object is converted into images, concepts, and words, which can only attend to parts of the whole and, moreover, to only those parts that are, to an extent, already known. In its pieced-together structure, Schafer's work reflects and reenacts the psychic trials that we undergo before it.

The imagination, that faculty of ours that is charged with generating images—as though "out of the blue," *sui generis*—should have no say in this closed circuit of exchange but, here at least, it would appear that it does. Accordingly, one might want to approach the work somewhat like a Rorschach Blot that not only causes the imaginative process of free association, but also encodes the effects of this process. What is it? When the question is posed by a psychoanalyst, the only wrong answer would be the right one: "It is a Rorschach Blot." In the psychiatric context, the point is not to determine what the thing is in itself, but what it is to you, the analysand. For the specific purposes of this exercise, therefore, it would be better to ask: "What do you see in it?" Or even, as a preemptive strike on whatever it is in The Real that is blocking the way to The Imaginary: "What does the ink-blot resemble?" To put it this way is to come a little bit closer to the context of art, but we are not there yet, as art does not take sides. Rather, it asks us to keep both questions in mind throughout the course of analysis: "What is it (in itself)?" and "What does it look like (to you)?"

Let's imagine a being for whom the first question is simply unanswerable. This being would have to be a blank slate, totally oblivious to art and to life as well, having crashed to earth from a distant planet, let's say, without any knowledge of its nature and customs. Landing right outside the Huntington Hospital in Pasadena, California, the first thing it encounters is David Schafer's sculpture, *Separated United Forms* (2009), newly installed right between the parking lot and California Street. What is it? Either the form of this thing will be recognized, or not. We may assume that for an alien, as for ourselves, the first impression of this unknown thing will either fall in or fall out of registration with something else that is known.

In that interim period between knowing and not, we are granted some speculative leeway in regard to the facts "on the ground." Our alien would not necessarily understand the work as a work, let alone a work of art. As noted, this being might actually relate to it as another being, one that could then be compared to whatever it understands itself to be. By way of example, one might imagine a form of alien life that would not move through space and time as we do, but rather appear, all at once, in different locations while remaining perfectly still. If this alien being were also blob-like and made of metal, then the sculpture could appear to it as a kin. If not, it would instead appear alien, and consequently perhaps be construed as a representative form of terrestrial life. To think in this way is admittedly fanciful, but it is not without some justification.

Ignoring for a moment the sculpture's placement before the hospital, let's consider instead the fact that it stands between a parking structure, where cars are at rest, and the street, where they are in motion. This, combined with the observation that people rarely walk in Los Angeles and are more often seen behind the wheel of their vehicles, might lead to the assumption that earth is inhabited by cars rather than people. If humankind is only seen to exist inside the car, then, in the imagination at least, it can be subsumed to the car's internal machinery. Since the object in question conforms more to the scale of the cars that surround it than to the scale of the people inside those cars, it would not be unreasonable to see these two things as related. True, this particular thing bears only a *passing* resemblance to a car, but whatever perceptions of structural irregularity persist under these conditions can be explained as an effect of its liminal state. Caught between inside and out, motion and rest, the car-like quality of the thing may be suspended as merely provisional. Whatever it might be, then, it is still becoming.

The figure of the alien comes to mind only because Schafer's sculpture resembles one. That is, to a human observer, it is not only alien in the sense of being utterly unfathomable and unlikely, it also "looks like" an alien. The degree of its morphological divergence from all that is accepted by us as belonging to the natural world is the measure of its other-ness, but this other-ness also bears certain irrefutable markers of the same, and these answer instead to a homegrown cultural construction of alien life. For instance, one might catch in it a glimpse of the chaotically mutating creature from *The Blob*, that early-1960s conflation of Sci-Fi and JD (Juvenile Delinquent) genres, right along with its still-playful intimations of the postwar catastrophe of corporate over-reach and unchecked consumerism. Those who grew up in the period of the film's release will perhaps appreciate the way that the sculpture's biomorphism alludes to both the space-monster's abject condition and the sublime aspirations inherent in the film's small-town space-age milieu. These older viewers may experience the work's alternation between arbitrariness and determination, formlessness and form, as tensed, even anxious; whereas for the younger ones, all such contradictions will have been resolved already. Whether the alien is literally "not of this world" or a direct outcome of our technocratic assault on organic structure will become increasingly irrelevant to every next generation that emerges out of the second "Big Bang." Even an atom-age creature like Godzilla was still prone to side with children against the order of their elders, but in the wake of Pikachu—arguably, the closest pop-cultural cousin of the work on offer—the mutant no longer stands to indict anyone.

As the cultural references begin piling up, we have already traveled a long way from what might be termed an innocent encounter, which is what I had hoped to entertain with the figure of the lost alien. Obviously, one cannot understand the condition of alienation in anything but relative terms, or more to the point, in relation to what is not alien. Nevertheless, the assumption of a distanced and uninformed vantage on art is occasionally encouraged by the work itself, especially when it appears outside its proper context. When it is met outside "in the world," as this work is, then it asks to be judged in worldly, as well as aesthetic, terms. The aesthetic is that part of the work that is variable and, when it is sealed off from the givens of the outlying reality by the architectural framework of the gallery, this condition is raised to the level of an absolute. Inside the so-called "white cube," the work could be anything and yet it is this and only this. What is it? Here, the question is answered categorically: it is art. Outside, this crucial determination may be deferred for a moment.

B. I Don't Know, But...

So far, the work has been described as a singular thing even though it is, in the main, comprised of two discrete parts. Moreover, it is largely in response to this two-part composition that the theme of resemblance is raised in the first place, since these parts closely resemble each other. They share the same scale, the same general shape, the same material make-up, the same dark-gray/brown coloration and the same smooth matte surface. Each part is "all of one part," in the language of Donald Judd, meaning that it confronts us as a unified mass devoid of internal compositional relations; yet, at the same time, it is one that is inscribed throughout with subdividing striations in a way that recalls the chassis of older model cars, when these were molded from a single sheet of steel. The determined articulation of the work's surface might suggest an underlying bone structure and musculature that is animal-like. Accordingly, as with most animals, the unified quality of the exterior may come to be seen as a kind of skin, drawn taut over a multiplicity of parts inside. To extrapolate from the external givens, the disposition of the interior is to cross the threshold of appearance, to project; now one may conceive of the two parts of the work as belonging to the same genus or species, while remaining nevertheless distinct. The two parts of the work share the same parts, but in different combination, which gives rise to the thought that they are particular instances of a general type of creature. From a distance, at first glance, or in passing (as behind the wheel of a car), these two might appear to be mirroring one another. This impression stems from the vague sense that, first, they are standing, and second, they are standing face to face. Raised off the ground on foot-like extensions, they assume a particular posture in regard to each other that is evidently not relaxed, or not entirely so. As with larger mammals such as the bison, rhinoceros, or whale, one can begin to discern an enlarged front—what might be designated as the prow of the animal—that tapers off in back. In this way, front to front, they seem to be locked in confrontation, "facing off."

There are intimations of drama in the way the two parts of the work are configured. Were there only one, it would certainly be more disorienting to us and yet more stable in itself. A viewer might not be tempted to assign it a front and back at all; alone, it would be simply encountered as a curious shape. It is the two-part composition of the work that invites narrative in-reading, suggesting relations of attraction and/or repulsion, the push and pull of an elemental life-force, between them.

Linguistics tells us that repetition, doubling, is at the root of meaning-making. When one "wild sound" is followed by another just like it, that likeness signals the emergence of a structuring intent, a primal speech. Similarly, within psychoanalysis, it is telling that the onset of identity occurs before a mirror: in the so-called "mirror-stage," we observe an infant doubled by its reflection, joined into one by splitting in two. The sound repeated, like the figure reflected, enters into the symbolic order as a re-presentation. The aforementioned Rorschach Blot is founded on a similar principle, which is why it furnishes us with such an apt analogy to Schafer's sculpture. Whatever one imagines it is and/or appears to be, this much is clear: it has to do with communication.

We can arrive at this conclusion without identifying the object in question as a work of art, and it might even be preferable not to do so just yet, as this would certainly limit the range of our speculations on and around it. However, at this point, we have already assumed it to be a work of some sort and therefore something that did not arise organically up from the earth or fall magically down from the sky. The moment we recognize that our object is made to mean, we are no longer able to freely project onto it any meaning we wish. This thing is now charged with a communicative agency that some may find threatening.

C. I Do Know, But...

Those who know what art is, but only in the most rudimentary sense—stopping far short of developing any authentic interest in the matter—will at least understand the work in question as a type of public sculpture. They will be able to read the cues that determine its status as such: that it stands beside a large public building where people from all parts of the city come and go; that it stands outside in the open, available to all, but without serving any obvious purpose; that it stands there "honorifically," set apart from the surrounding grass on a neat rectangle of smooth concrete that has been embedded, here and there, with spotlight fixtures to illuminate it at night; that it stands at a scale that may be described as "heroic," smaller than the buildings around it, yet larger than the people that move about those buildings; that it stands still, having been made of metal, and moreover of bronze, the emblematic material of public sculpture, which we experience as weighty, immovable, permanent. On every count, Schafer's work conforms to our expectations of what public sculpture generally is. As to what it might be more specifically, however, the work will prove more resistant.

No doubt, it is due to the sense that it will outlast us that public sculpture can still provoke a public otherwise largely indifferent to art. An enduring aspect is implicit in all works, but here it is explicitly declared, and it is precisely the public nature of this declaration, addressed as it is to one and all, that can rub the wrong way. We all have a stake in what will outlast us, as this also is what we collectively bequeath to the coming generations: our cultural legacy. Schafer's sculpture may strike some as deficient in this respect, since it does not commemorate, ennoble, or redeem any part of our experience in such a way as to prepare it for history. Instead, it simply stays put; it "stands its ground"—I want to say, tauntingly, even if this applies only to those who are put off by it—without standing for anything in particular.

Those who have dutifully submitted their critiques to the local press exercise their knowledge of what art is only to determine what it is not. In order to declare something inartistic, that is, one must first be able to recognize it as a work of art. Accordingly, Schafer's sculpture has been derided as ugly and stupid, a dismal assessment that simultaneously denies it the possibility of being conceptually knowing in regard to its form and unknowingly formal. In this way, whatever it is or appears to be can be dismissed as accidental, as when one observer pronounced the work a "turd." Others have assumed the problem with it to be entirely intended, a "slap in the face," as when one particular observer peered "through" the perplexing shapes of Schafer's sculpture and made out heaps of fat, and by extension, a mean-spirited swipe at the obese. The artist told me about a woman who went so far as to charge the Pasadena Arts Council with obscenity, seeing the work as a grotesque compendium of sexual organs and nothing else. None of these interpretations is necessarily wrong since, as mentioned, the work is as amenable as a Rorschach Blot to our various projections, whatever these might consist of.

Having identified the work in question as a type of public sculpture, we may now give that type a name: abstraction. Here, again, the determination is made on the basis of the work's divergence from all that is known and familiar to us, but within this difference, something must also be recognized. It does not *exactly* resemble anything under the sun except for one thing, and that is abstract sculpture in the most general sense. This point might not be fully appreciated by an only partly informed audience, who will tend to approach abstraction in a manner that is either more open (it could be anything) or closed (it is this and only this). For this segment of the public, abstraction is either conducive to the free play of the imagination or more like a problem to solve. Feces, fat, sex-organs—all of these answer the question "What is it?" in terms of "What does it look like to you?" without accounting for the possibility of difference between them. A more dialectical approach will help us avoid the extremes of over-estimation and under-estimation that come with this "middle-brow" territory, where abstraction can only be judged wholly original or else wholly derivative, but never self-

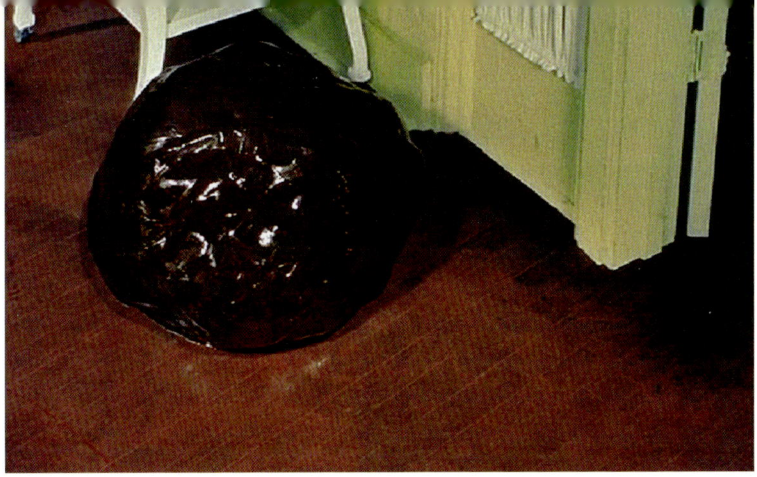

Still from *The Blob*, 1958

knowing in regard to its history and present-day circumstance.

And yet there remains a vague suspicion that the sculpture "itself" actually does know something and perhaps even knows more than you do. Those that have felt compelled to vent publicly on and about this public work may well be airing an authentic grievance in this regard. Within their angry words one can detect a kind of anxiety that cannot be confined to any one work in particular but, rather, takes in abstraction in general, the very existence of which is somehow deemed to be personally insulting. It is as a generic example of abstract art that Schafer's work is taken to task by this public, provoking an outcry that those among us who are more analytically disinterested may find utterly disproportionate to what it is more specifically.

The vehemence of this response reveals much more about the subject than the object in question, but this does not make it wrong. As noted, what we are considering here is a public work of abstract sculpture that resembles many different things to many different people, and this is because it resembles no one thing exactly. Even if it is to be categorized as abstract rather than figurative, it is not in a way that would resolve the problem it poses to us once and for all, as it only inclines more to one side than the other by a few degrees. This difference is not really one of a kind; even to those who are more favorably inclined toward abstract sculpture in general, this particular work will still only *look like* the abstraction one might want it to be—in the sense of being so fully, autonomously, and thereby released from likeness altogether. Even here, among a somewhat more informed public of "art lovers," there persists a nagging perception that the work remains either too open or closed. This shape-shifting function is integral to its design as an analytical object: it can be anything to anyone, but this is not to suggest that it is in itself anything, that it is unmotivated and arbitrary—to the contrary.

D. I Do Know, And...

As we transition from not-knowing to knowing, our interpretation of the work will not necessarily gain in accuracy, as accuracy is rather a matter of representation. To measure the degree of overlap between a representational word and a presentational thing, one must first assume that they exist apart, which is exactly what we have so far avoided. Again, our object is analytical; it is, from the outset, comprised as much of word-things as thing-words.

With respect to what it is or appears to be, feces, fat and sex-organs may strike us as highly subjective interpretations—and they are, but that is not all that they are. Even as expressions of a woefully under-examined subconscious, all of the above demonstrate some sensitivity at least to the objective fact of the sculpture's siting. Here, the response actually meets with the artist's own expectations, as it is not for nothing that Schafer placed his work on the grounds of a hospital, a building where stool samples are in fact taken, body weight measured, and private parts exposed.

As mentioned, Schafer was schooled in the early 1980s when, under the influence of postmodern theory, artistic practices were formulated in direct critical opposition to the modern and to its ideal of autonomous abstract form. On this point, as well, a tacit agreement may be noted between the artist and the most hostile segment of his audience: neither side can be counted among abstraction's "true-believers." Moreover, both consider abstraction a historical convention already, one wholly implicated in the so-called "dominant order" and compromised by it and all its attendant institutions—and thereby not really autonomous at all. Every attack on the work only reinforces the critical assumptions that underwrite it, demonstrating the downside of autonomy as a modernist ideal of inner-aesthetic self-sufficiency and outward indifference, both of which are now as vulnerable to critique as the thing-in-itself. In this way, as well, the work can be seen as both the cause and effect of what we do before it; for one cannot recognize it as an abstraction without also contending with the thought of failure, even disaster, as it pertains to the abstracted object as much as the abstracted subject—that is, oneself.

This work of abstract art has been placed outside a hospital; there it awaits our diagnosis. Depending on who delivers it, this diagnostic will tend to vary, but on one point all agree: it is grim. Inasmuch as the work relates to the body—to its public and private presentation and representation, to its perceived outside and inside, to its objective relation to the knowing and unknowing subject, to its condition from the perspective of both life and art (which must also take into account whatever bearing the one might have on the other)—it is clear that this is a body in crisis. The word "crisis" furnishes the etymological link between diagnosis and critique and, here at least, lends to its exercise a palpable urgency. By any estimation, this is an unstable body. It is changing, and due to its placement on the hospital grounds, one must assume that it is not changing for the better.

It is certainly paradoxical that such a work, which is made of enduring and timeless bronze to suit the category of the abstract public sculpture in the most conventional sense, should come fraught with intimations of abject impermanence. One would not be prone to fantasizing so anxiously before a sculpture by Henry Moore, for instance, and so it is even more paradoxical that it is in fact Moore who has provided Schafer with the model for this form. Moore, the post-war exemplar of the civic sculptor, a "master" of what is now known, not without derision, as "soft modernism," is at the root of the work "at hand." To put it glibly, one could say that Schafer's handling of this art historical precedent comes down to a joke, as it works to make literal the softness of Moore's modernism. Here, once again, the artist appears to be siding with his anti-art opposition, but jokes are supposed to make us laugh, and no such release is to be gained from this particular work.

To preclude the release of laughter is possibly the most deliberate thing that Schafer has done here, for no matter where one stands on the scale between knowing and not, there is no privileged vantage from which anything like a punch-line can be received. In this regard, those who do not even see the work as a work, let alone a work of art, are really no wiser than those who do. Those who believe that abstract art is a joke on them and those who believe that the joke is rather on abstract art will remain to the end equally oblivious as to what this joke might actually be, if it even is a joke. We have determined that Schafer's original inspiration is a work by Henry Moore, an all-too appropriate and hence somewhat humorous source for a work of abstract public sculpture. But unlike the treatment that he received at the hands of Martin Kippenberger, for instance, who pushed Moore's empathetic distortions of natural form into the realm of outright bathos in his *Familie Hunger* (The Hunger Family, 1985), Schafer steers clear of caricature. His stake in the matter of modernism as historical inheritance is more measured, nuanced and, at the same time, more speculative.

As it happens, Schafer pulled his model—*Reclining Form* is its title: this much is stated on the plaque that accompanies *Separated United Forms*—from the collection of the Norton Simon Museum of Art, which, not incidentally, is close to where his work winds up once finished. In its original form, the chosen Henry Moore sculpture assumes the table-top scale of a modest sculptural sketch, relatively free of the existential-heroic associations conjured up by his best-known works. Certainly, one will also find some humor in the scale shift that it undergoes in the process of translation, but much more significant are its inner-aesthetic compositional shifts. Transitioning between the Norton Simon Museum and the Huntington Hospital, the chosen Moore first had to pass through another civic portal, this one virtual. Scanned inside the museum vault by Art Center College of Design's digital technician under guarded view by security officers and the curatorial staff, its sculptural form was encoded as information. It is the virtual ghost of this emphatically actual, hand-made thing that was then recomposed, by Schafer, into something very different. The resulting digital files were next brought to the Machine Histories facility in Los Angeles, where further sampling and 3D modeling was performed in preparation for the mold making and casting process of the finished work at the Walla Walla Foundry. There is some humor in this as well, and it follows through the entire cycle of production: Schafer's reworked Henry Moore is at last re-turned, as a dematerialized data, to the foundry, its place of origin, where it is rematerialized as a bronze sculpture.

The play between these two contexts, the digital lab and the foundry, is pointed in regard to our ostensibly post-industrial moment, emphasizing what Marx designates as "non-synchronous" in all historical experience. The uneven development of productive forces and their corresponding social relations is simply a given within the context of art, though it is often overshadowed by the allure of "The New." Not here: Schafer's sculpture takes its problematic shape at the juncture of the new-fangled and the old-fashioned. Both qualities are evident in the form of the work, neither one predominating.

Past and future tenses are layered upon it as sedimented deposits of a voyage that has taken it from a space of artistic reception (museum), via art school, to a space of artistic production (foundry). That the work's final destination (hospital) has nothing intrinsically to do with art at all is what keeps this narrative from simply turning back on itself in a way that would resolve it for those of us "in the know."

It has not been made only for us; this much is evident in the work's siting as much as its form, which is, as mentioned, two-part. These two parts describe a relation that is dynamic, perhaps even dramatic, but one that, as sculpture, is also inherently static. If, as suggested, these parts can be understood as entities frozen in an act of mutual observation, it cannot be ascertained whether they do or do not recognize one another. This "face off," and the indeterminacy that enfolds it, allegorically mirrors our precarious encounter with the work of art and, through this work, with ourselves and each other.

E. All of the Above

A disclaimer: as this essay begins to approach its conclusion, I want to counter any expectations of a final reveal. This is not the place to correct "the error of our ways" in regard to all that has been covered already in the way of analysis. The assumption that there actually does exist a single right answer to the question asked of us—what is it?—belongs only to those who have remained faithful to the cult of the author as the keeper of the hermeneutic key, the "last word" on what it is. Even so, what if this author had *intentionally* surrendered any such hold over the meaning of his work? What if this author had *intentionally* ceded the privilege of authorship to his audience? One might now assume that, in the interest of analysis, "anything goes," and consequently seize upon "all of the above" as the answer that trumps all the others. It would certainly not be wrong to do so, but this does not necessarily make it right.

The two parts of the work are derived from a single whole that appeared, to Schafer, to be splitting apart somewhat like a cell or an atom is split. With the assistance of computer technology, the artist simply carried this process of splitting through to its end, drawing two discrete forms out of the one. These resulting forms are at once same and other, comprising a related set of physical traits but in different combination. Whatever the work might look like to you, this at least can be declared objectively: it consists of two parts that look like each other, but not entirely. And it is entirely due to the perception of a general resemblance between them that we come to understand these two parts as non-identical in the particular. Because there are two, the analysis that follows will have to be comparative, deflected from the thing in itself to a relation between things. As with a pair of twins, or even clones, one impulsively scans the two parts for signs of divergence. One would like to deliver the verdict that would break their stalemate: declaring one side more right, more just, and/or more beautiful than the other.

In order to diagnose the condition of a body, one must have recourse to a standard of health, and much the same goes for the work of art. Whether it is considered individually, or else collectively—and these terms are telling: as a "body of work," an aesthetic "corpus"—the measure of art's ill-health can only be taken against a standard of well-being. If, in the postwar years, so many artists in the West embraced abstraction as a means of radical reduction, purging their art of all but the essentially organic, it was in pursuit of just such a standard. Here, it is recognized that the first casualty of war had been mankind's own self-image and that to restore this self-image must therefore be a first priority in any plan for reconstruction. The challenge to re-humanize the experience of art is echoed on all sides of the cultural debate in response to the dehumanization of war, but nowhere is it met more directly than in the studio of Henry Moore, whose entire practice boils down to whatever it is that constitutes the living nature of the living thing. To distill the vital life-principle into concrete form is a general aim of "art throughout the ages," but in the post-war years it takes on a particular urgency, for here it also implies the search for a cure to what ails us.

For Moore and his contemporaries, the well-being of art remains essentially bound up with the well-being of nature, and it is by way of abstraction that the artist works through the appearance of natural life to its innermost "rule," as Immanuel Kant would say. This "rule" is derived from the organic signature that lies embedded deep inside the substance of all living things, hidden behind appearance, which is presented to us as its superficial effect, while also providing a clue as to its cause. In much the same way that seedling becomes a tree, for instance, abstract form is developed as the outward expression of an inner-aesthetic command that issues from somewhere between the material, the tools of the making, and the maker himself.

The artist who has become fluent in reading right through the protective shell of the object world to its living core will have found there the essential formula of form as such.

Any such effort aspires to a condition of timelessness almost by definition, and it is one that, now more than ever perhaps, must itself be seen as date-stamped. It is entirely as a "sign of the times" that Moore's work is taken up here, his post-war pursuit of organic essence as the shared ground of being no longer sealed off from the social as an inner-aesthetic imperative, but responding directly to the threat of a society evidently governed by the death-drive. In Schafer's reworking, that is, the holistic form of Moore's organic symbol comes apart in the shadow of a spreading mushroom cloud.

From one into two: this is the first stage in a process of identity formation that has here taken a pathological turn. The characteristics of the same and the other are distributed in equal proportion on either side of the East/West divide; whatever difference can still be made out between them is rather a matter of more or less arbitrary recombination. The two parts of Schafer's sculpture enact their standoff in a manner that might recall the frozen Cold War posture of two great super-powers, both of them other only in regard to each other while remaining essentially same in themselves.

The various doubles considered so far—the repeated "wild sound," the reprinted ink blot, the reflected figure in the mirror—may also be termed non-identical, but in a very different way, and this is because they all come second to what may then be recognized as the first, the original, the "real thing." Here, no such distinction can be made: neither part is fuller, thicker, sharper, or more present than the other. There is no way to tell between presence and representation on the basis of compression, loss, or corruption. The two parts of Schafer's work remain identically non-identical, locked in place and time like a joke endlessly awaiting its punch-line.

It was Freud who suggested that jokes level the wall between thoughts previously understood as incompatible. As what was imagined to be alien is revealed to be the familiar in effect, the polarized structure of identity is itself momentarily confounded, which leads to a physical convulsion of the subjective interior—laughter—as it is assailed by what lies outside its bounds. In this way, jokes can be said to operate not unlike art in that both seek to confront us with something else, something that we do not already know. And it is on this point that Schafer's work remains utterly intractable: the wall is left standing precisely because we have already recognized what lies on the opposite side as the same, only perhaps more so.

F. None of the Above

This, the final section of my essay, is really an extension of the previous one, and so the same disclaimer applies. Here, again, the question that we began with—What is it?—will not find an answer that is any more accurate or erroneous than any other. To opt for the surplus of meaning in "all of the above" is not necessarily so different from the lack of meaning in "none of the above." A work that means different things to different people is one that could potential-ly mean anything and, by the same token, nothing. A work so open and inviting to interpretation, so potentially full of meaning, is also potentially meaningless.

If we agree that this work is at the very least ambivalent with respect to its meaning, then it is also potentially unmotivated, arbitrary. It could be anything, as mentioned, and yet it is this and only this. Its form is particular and determined to the nth degree, which raises the question of just what it is particular and determined about. At this point, one might entertain the possibility that form is here being asserted in opposition to meaning, that the work is about sensibility rather than sense, but that would not be exactly right either, since it is neither quite "formal" nor unformed, *informel*. Here, again, it is in the repetition of its two-part structure that this work counters any inclination on the part of the reader to default toward the purely aesthetic. If there were any more parts, these might begin to suggest between them a structural play of theme and variation, but between only two parts the margin for play narrows down to a line. A line in the sand: the two parts are locked in confrontation, an epic showdown to which the free play of aesthetic form is necessarily surrendered.

The "jubilation" that Lacan observes taking hold of the infant before his mirror image is here decisively quashed. Whatever drama is suggested between the two parts of Schafer's sculpture, their relation cannot be confined to an expression of sheer physicality; they are much too inert, heavy, and ponderous for that. If it has to do with the "mirror stage" at all, then it is in a way that must take in as well the critical eye of the analyst. That physicality is here presented

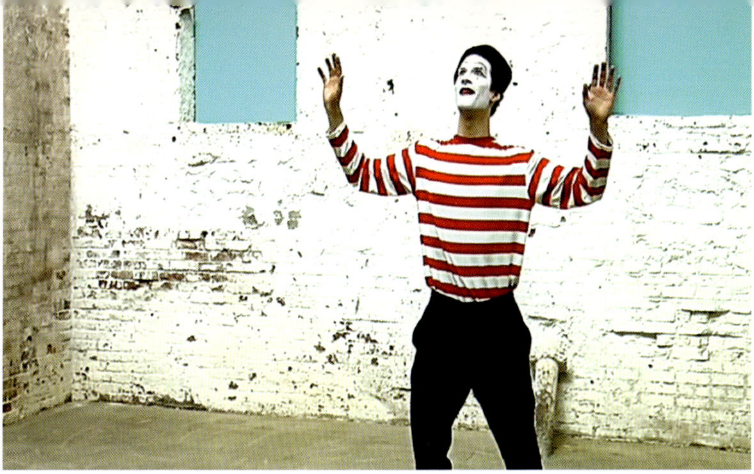

Still from *Choreography for Mime: Making a Sculpture,* 2009

as something to read is confirmed by the work's two-part structure, which can be read accordingly as demonstrating just such a reading. The resemblance that we note between these parts is an effect of this reading, as are their various points of divergence. In their imperfect physical mimicry of one another, we can read the relativity of meaning, the arbitrariness of the sign as well as the absolute determination of the system within which it operates.

A prior public art project, executed by Schafer in Cadman Plaza in Brooklyn Heights, Brooklyn, New York, in 1988, prepares us to read this one as being all about its reading. Its title, *Plaza of the First Reader,* instantly directs the passerby away from a purely sensual encounter with the work and toward the realm of the intellect. More pointedly still, it affirms the centrality of the reader within its structural make-up, both as a built thing and a staged experience. Consisting of a shallow round podium, partially encircled by a railing and stuck in the middle with a tall pole, it offers one precious little to work with that is concretely sculptural. Rather, as with so many of Schafer's works from this period, its constituent forms are revealed, on closer inspection, to be made out of language. The podium is inscribed with the letter "e"; the pole hoists up the letter "b"; further down the road,

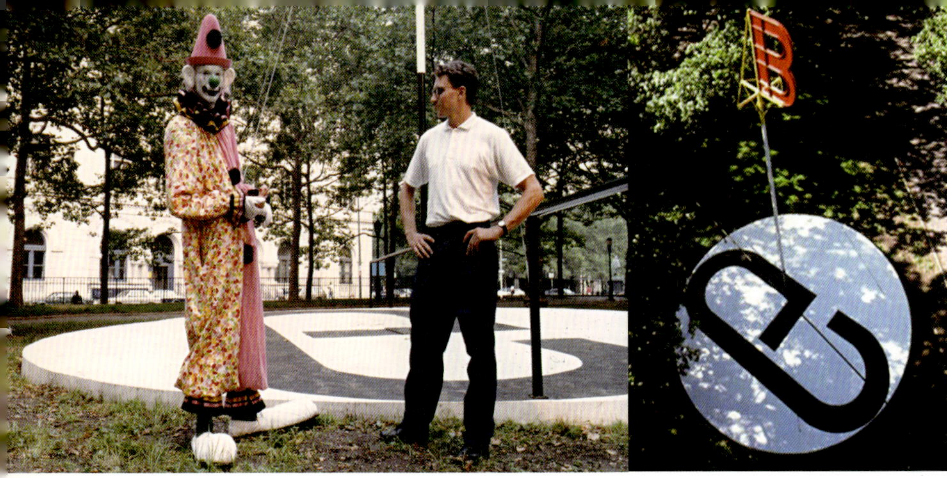

David Schafer with clown, and detail of *Plaza of the First Reader*, 1988, Brooklyn, New York

other signposts are encountered bearing the letters "s," "e," and "e" ("see"), and then "s," "a," and "y" ("say"). Together, these letterforms and words ("say," "see," and "be") prime us to read the work as a reading lesson in public sculpture that therefore cannot also be the sculptural thing in itself.

What, then, is this work? Or, better still, where and when does it happen? Inasmuch as *Plaza of the First Reader* is both of and about public sculpture, it asks us to consider the question from two sides: that of production and reception. The being of it ("be") must somehow be grasped through the seeing of it ("see") as an articulation, a saying of it that would hold equally true for the artist/author as the viewer/reader. With great precision, Schafer's work marks the spot where this confluence is supposed to, but ultimately cannot, occur. As if to drive home the point, a clown was hired to casually wander about the grounds on the opening day as an acutely unstable stand-in for both parties on either side of the production/reception stand-off.

There is good reason to believe that Schafer is "clowning around," as he has done so before, but as even the most casual reader of the "social sciences" will understand, clowning is always also a serious matter. Many, or most, of the questions raised in his latest work have appeared in previous ones: questions pertaining specifically to public art, to its siting, its audience, and its social function. More generally, as well, Schafer has approached the question of abstraction as a question before, not so much to work through it in search of an answer, but to keep the question itself in play within the finished form of the work. Questionable abstraction, one might want to call it as a somewhat more humorous designation for what we have so far considered in terms of the analytical object. The humor in it stems from an evident redundancy, since, in the eyes of the general public at least, abstract art is always already in question. However, it is largely because Schafer assumes this questionable status as an *a priori*—a cause rather than an effect of abstraction—that his works stand apart from, and in opposition to, those they resemble. Time and again, with mounting insistence, the figure of the clown is reintroduced into the experiential equation of abstract art as a questionable stand-in for both the artist and public. In linguistic terms, he would be a "shifter" capable of representing both sides in their stand-off, but without in any way resolving it. To the contrary, the clown effectively embodies the worst suspicions on either side as to the nature of the other: the artist as joker, having a laugh at the expense of the public, which is accordingly cast in the role of the fool.

The painted-on hyper-expressionism of the circus clown is drastically subdued on the face of the mime, a hypo-expressionist who mirrors only the outward form of our actions. Schafer has employed both of these figures in his work as a sort of bracketing device, marking out the extreme points of meaningful surplus and meaningless lack, while at the same time conflating them. Whereas the circus clown is only invited to attend the opening of *Plaza of the First Reader*, the mime is charged with the work's execution in *Choreography for a Mime: Making a Sculpture* (2009). Because he can only mime it, however, the work itself must be imagined as always already made and, at the same time, essentially unmakeable.

In a loosely defined series of works begun in 2002 and basically ongoing, titled Untitled Expression, Schafer draws from the oeuvre of The Three Stooges an emblematic instance of questionably abstract sculpture, one that is in fact made by the clown. As it appears in the 1938 episode "How High Is Up?" this thing assumes sculptural form only by failing to work as architecture, which is what the Stooges had originally been contracted to build. The utterly dysfunctional mess of crisscrossing I-Beams that results is extruded from the film by Schafer, first as a still image and then as a small-scale construction of welded steel. This in turn becomes the model for a succession of larger-scale works (Untitled Expression, 1 through 13) that bear a resemblance to the work of Anthony Caro from the start, but cross over into outright mimicry by the end, as their metallic grid-work structure is treated to a powder-coated finish of primary color.

From a poster produced to accompany a show of closely related problem objects, a black-and-white portrait of Curly stares out at us with chin firmly balanced on fist, eyes narrowed, expression inscrutable. Whereas the circus clown "wears his face" in a permanent grimace of joy or sadness, this Stooge confronts us blankly. In the art context into which he has been inserted, such po-faced looks are

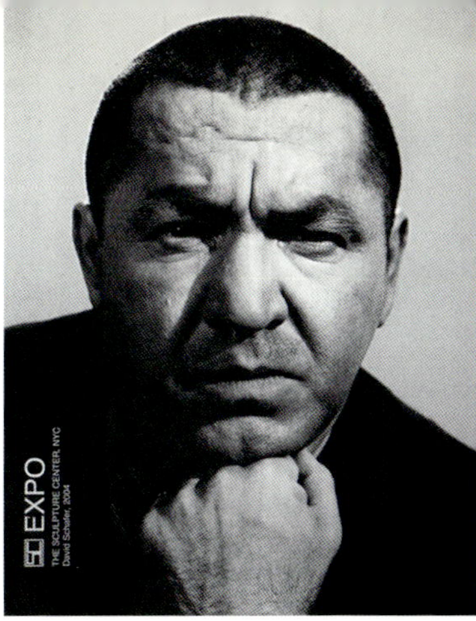

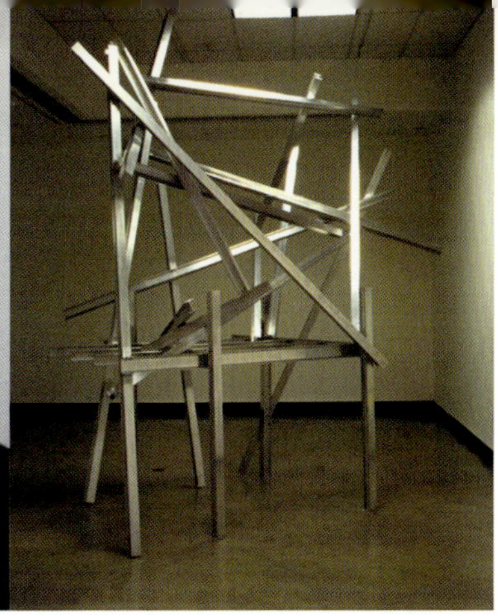

David Schafer, *High is Up How?*, 2005. "ReModeling," Art Museum of Long Beach, California

General Theory poster for "Treble," 2004. Sculpture Center, Long Island City, New York

de rigeur, generating the requisite distance to keep earnestness from tipping into naivety. Such a look would ideally confirm the credibility of the expression within the work without exceeding and replacing it. It is a classic "serious man" picture, except that it is Curly, and we know this man to be unserious in the extreme. He could be giving himself a stiff upper-cut, thereby actively emptying out the mind behind this mask of "the thinker."

Here, again, we can think about mirroring. The head of Curly reflects the heads that come before it, seeking there a stable grounding source for the work in question, a proper author, only to be confronted instead with just another reader. If this face-off of mutually suspicious in-reading—"I know that you know that I know..."—can only devolve into an empty-headed staring contest, then it is one where Curly, or rather his photographic likeness, clearly has the advantage, and much the same can be said for the work on view. A misbegotten architecture executed by clowns and then "redeemed" by Schafer as modernist sculpture, it also greets us blankly. In its *de rigeur* titling as Untitled, it exudes the same vague provocation as Curly's expressionless face, which may now be seen to operate as an aggressive negation of the expression that we had hoped to find

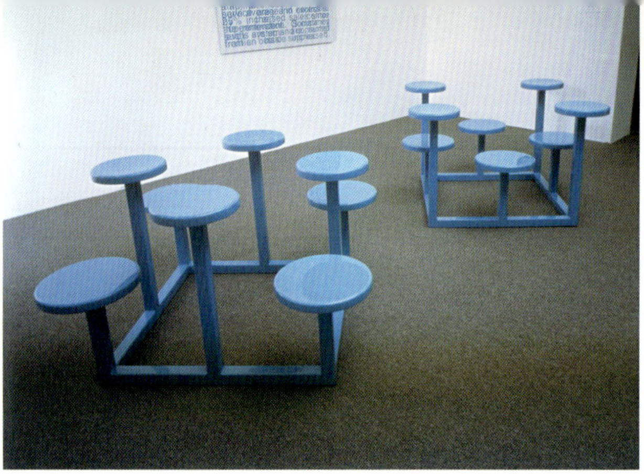

Installation view of *Stepped Density*, in "Body Space," 2001, Baltimore Museum, Baltimore, Maryland

there. *Untitled Expression* connects the dots between The Three Stooges and Anthony Caro, and there is a whole series of these, numbered between one and thirteen. Differentiated by scale, material, and color, these retain the same compositional structure throughout, never coming any closer to giving that expression a name.

To return one last time to *Separated United Forms* via this detour, we must transition from the rectilinear geometric abstraction of Caro to the curvilinear organic abstraction of Moore. Between these two references there lies a whole world of difference, but in Schafer's reworkings it is narrowed down to a line. The same line that runs through each individual work also runs between them, giving rise to a general perception of two-sidedness and an idea of a resemblance that is non-identical inasmuch as every trait that is shared on either side has also been flipped. Reversal is the first sign of difference in the mirror image, and from it further signs may be seen to emerge, the reflection and its source gradually locking together in a feedback loop of dysmorphia. Schafer has followed this process from start to end in *Separated United Forms*. It is effectively what he is composing, both from the inside out and the outside in.

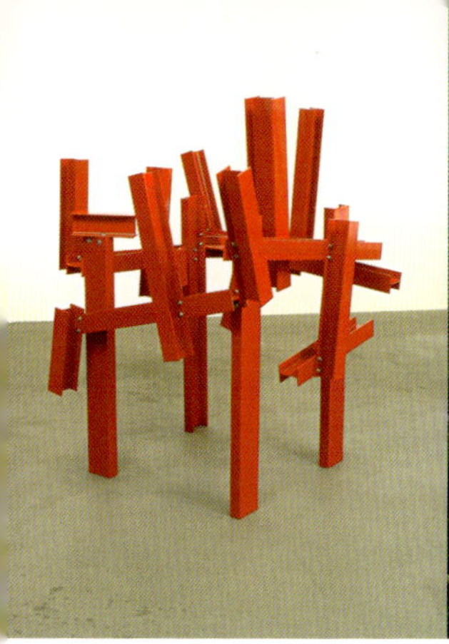

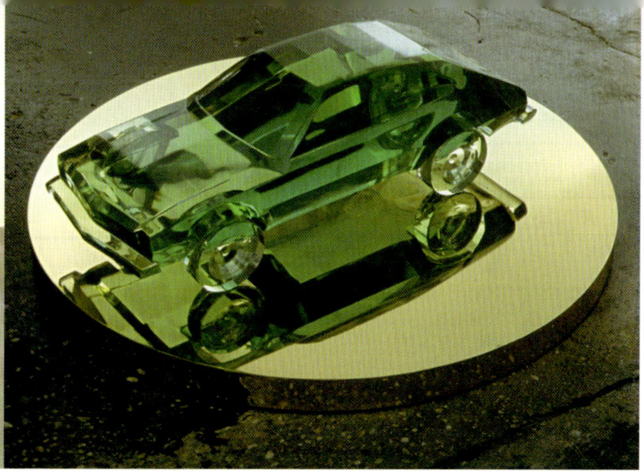

The Double Illusion of the Mystic Linguistic Event, 2001, courtesy Sara Meltzer Gallery, New York

David Schafer, *Untitled Expression #3: Red*, 2005

Notes

1 Friedrich Kittler, *Gramophone, Film, Typewriter,* trans. Geoffrey Winthrop-Young & Michael Wutz (Stanford, California: Stanford University Press, 1999), 7.

2 See Roland Barthes, "From Work to Text," in *Image, Music, Text,* trans. Stephen Heath (New York, New York: Hill and Wang, 1977), 155-164; and Michel Foucault, "What is an Author?," in *Language, Counter-Memory, Practice,* trans. Donald F. Bouchard and Sherry Simon (Ithaca, New York: Cornell University Press, 1977), 124–127.

CREDITS

pp. 2–3	Wire frame Separated United Forms (SUF); photo courtesy Jason Pilarski
p. 4	Examination Room, Huntington Hospital; photo courtesy Huntington Hospital, Pasadena, California
p. 6-7	Waiting Room, Huntington Outpatient Pavilion; photo courtesy Huntington Hospital
p. 8	Imaging and body scanning, Huntington Hospital; photo courtesy Huntington Hospital
p. 10	Internet stock image
p. 11	Photo courtesy Walla Walla Foundry, Walla Walla, Washington
p. 12	Photo courtesy of Huntington Hospital
p. 13	Internet stock image
pp. 14–15	Photo courtesy David Schafer
p. 16	Photo courtesy David Schafer
p. 17	Photo courtesy David Schafer
pp. 20	Henry Moore's Reclining Form in the process of being scanned, Norton Simon Museum, Pasadena, California; photo courtesy David Schafer
pp. 22–23	Henry Moore, Reclining Form, 1966; photo courtesy Norton Simon Museum
pp. 24–25	Art Center technician and Jason Pilarski scanning Henry Moore's Reclining Form at the Norton Simon Museum; photo courtesy David Schafer
p. 26	Slices; photo courtesy Jason Pilarski, Machine Histories
p. 26	Point cloud; photo courtesy Jason Pilarski, Machine Histories
p. 27	Triangular polygons, photo courtesy Jason Pilarski, Machine Histories
p. 31	Patch model; photo courtesy Jason Pilarski, Machine Histories
p. 32	Three Axis Mill, Machine Histories; photo courtesy David Schafer
p. 32	SUF Model being milled, Machine Histories; David Schafer
pp. 34–35	SUF Wire Frame; photo courtesy Jason Pilarski, Machine Histories
pp. 36–37	SUF Foam Model, Machine Histories; photo courtesy David Schafer
pp. 38–39	SUF 3D PNG Model, Machine Histories; photo courtesy Jason Pilarski
pp. 40–41	SUF Foam Model, exterior view; photo courtesy David Schafer
p. 42	SUF revealing superimposed forms; photo courtesy Jason Pilarski, Machine Histories
pp. 45–53	SUF Section Schematic; photo courtesy Dylan Farnum, Walla Walla Foundry
p. 54	SUF Molds, Walla Walla Foundry; photo courtesy David Schafer
pp. 56–57	SUF Mold Section, Walla Walla Foundry; photo courtesy David Schafer
pp. 58–59	SUF Wax Section, Walla Walla Foundry; photo courtesy David Schafer
pp. 60–61	SUF Wax Section with sprues and vents, Walla Foundry; photo courtesy David Schafer
pp. 62–63	SUF Wax Sections with ceramic shell coating, Walla Walla Foundry; photo courtesy David Schafer
p. 64	SUF Fabrication; photo courtesy Amahra Leaman, Walla Walla Foundry
pp. 65–71	SUF Fabrication; photo courtesy Amahra Leaman, Walla Walla Foundry
p. 72	Patination, Walla Walla Foundry; photo courtesy David Schafer
p. 74	Patination, Karl Longin, Walla Walla Foundry; photo courtesy David Schafer
p. 75	Patination, Todd Telander, Walla Walla Foundry; photo courtesy David Schafer
pp. 76–77	Patination, Walla Walla Foundry; photo courtesy David Schafer
pp. 78–79	Patination, Walla Walla Foundry; photo courtesy David Schafer
p. 80	Site Plan; photo courtesy of HDR Architecture, Inc., Omaha, Nebraska
p. 81	Body Imaging Machine; photo courtesy of Huntington Hospital
pp. 82–85	SUF Installation Detail; photo courtesy Eric Staudenmaier

p. 91 Photo courtesy David Schafer
p. 100 Photo courtesy Paramount Pictures
p. 113 Photo courtesy David Schafer
p. 114 Photo courtesy David Schafer
p. 114 Photo courtesy David Schafer
p. 117 Photo courtesy David Schafer
p. 118 Photo courtesy David Schafer
p. 119 Photo courtesy David Schafer
p. 119 Photo courtesy David Schafer
p. 127 SUF installation views; photo courtesy Eric Staudenmaier

Cover: Photo courtesy Jason Pilarski, Machine Histories
End pages: Photo courtesy Jason Pilarski, Machine Histories
Backcover: Photo courtesy Jason Pilarski, Machine Histories

Note: We apologize if, due to reasons wholly beyond our control, some of the photo sources have not been listed.

CREDITS

Pacific Medical Buildings
Bob Davidson, Development Consultant
Jim Rohan, Sr. V.P. Development
Loni Rush, Director of Design

Art Center College of Design
Laurence Dreiband, Department Chair, Fine Art
Frank Ellsworth, Interim-President, Art Center College of Design
Iris Gelt, Senior Vice President, Marketing/Communications
Jered Gold, Acting Director, Public Relations/Communications
Nikolaus Hafermass, Department Chair, Graphic Design
Leslie Marcus, Director, Special Programs
Jason Pilarski, Faculty, Digital Media
Michael Plesh, Director of Technical Services
David Walker, Dean of Public Programs

Department of Cultural Affairs: Art Commission of Pasadena
Rochelle Branch, Director, Art Program
Rebecca Deo, Interim Public Art Program Manager
Pauline Kamiyama, Public Art Program Coordinator

Norton Simon Museum
Andrea Clark Luna, Registrar
Javier Ramirez, Academic Intern
Carol Togneri, Chief Curator

Henry Moore Foundation
Suzanne Eustace, Assistant Curator
Emma Stower, Assistant Curator

HDR Architecture
Ara Sookazian, Senior Project Designer

Machine Histories
Steven Joyner, Principal Partner MH
Jason Pilarski, Principal Partner MH

Walla Walla Foundry
Mark Anderson, Owner
David Anderson, Director of Operations
Dylan Farnum, Director of Special projects
Amahra Leaman, Photographer
Jeremy Lilwall, Wax and Patina Specialist
Karl Longin, Patina Department
Jesus Mendoza, Production Supervisor, Metal Shop
Byron Peterson, Production Supervisor, Metal Shop
Shiloh Stot, Bronze Casting Specialist

Landscaping
Elizabeth Duer, Troller Mayer Associates, Inc
Richard W. Mayer ASLA, Troller Mayer Associates, Inc

Conservation
John Griswold, Griswold Conservation Associates, LLC

Lighting
Paul Fedors, Specification Outdoor Sales Manager
Harry Heard, Hydrel Product Specialist

Huntington Hospital
Connie Matthews, Director of Marketing/Communications
Clara Pacheco, MPI Facility Manager
Andrea Straddling, Public Relations

New York Studio
Rebecca Curry, Studio Assistant
Jess Ramsay, Studio Assistant

Los Angeles Studio
Jesse Gillan, Studio Assistant

Architecture Sign and Design
Maria Ableloff, Architectural Graphic Designer

Photography
Jean Rasenberger, Video
Eric Staudenmaier, Eric Staudenmaier Photography

Consultation
Mitchell Kane
Ed Suman, Carlson Fabrication

ACKNOWLEDGMENTS

The artist would like to gratefully acknowledge his family for their support and patience during the fabrication of the sculpture and production of the book.

This book was published in conjunction with the installation of *Separated United Forms* by David Schafer at the Huntington Pavilion in Pasadena, California.

Visual Design: Mitchell Kane, i-o-i-p.com
Editorial Consultation: Lisa Gabrielle Mark, material means
Technical Descriptions: David Anderson, Dylan Farnum, Karl Longin, Jason Pilarski
Essays: David Schafer, Jan Tumlir

Editorial Coordination
Daniela Meda, Filomena Moscatelli

Proofreading
Emily Ligniti

Copywriting and Press Office
Silvia Palombi

US Editorial Director
Francesca Sorace

Promotion and Web
Monica D'Emidio

Distribution
Antonia De Besi

Administration
Grazia De Giosa

Warehouse and Outlet
Roberto Curiale

ISBN 978-88-8158-794-0
Printed in 2010 by arti grafiche BIANCA&VOLTA, Truccazzano, Italy
for Edizioni Charta

Edizioni Charta srl
Milano
via della Moscova, 27 - 20121
Tel. +39-026598098/026598200
Fax +39-026598577
e-mail: charta@chartaartbooks.it

Charta Books Ltd.
New York City
Tel. +1-313-406-8468
e-mail: international@chartaartbooks.it

To find out more about Charta, and to learn about our more recent publications, visit
www.chartaartbooks.it

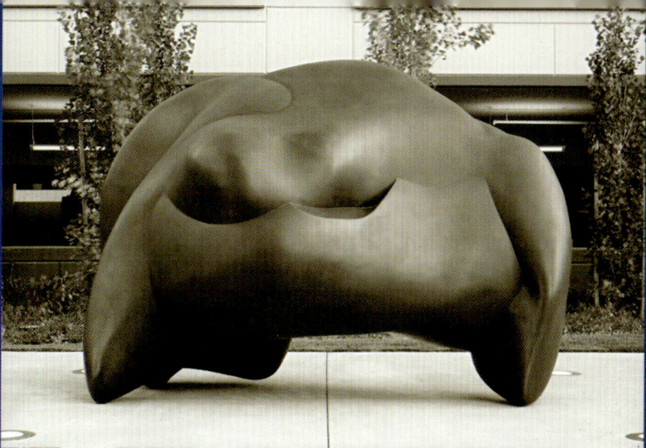

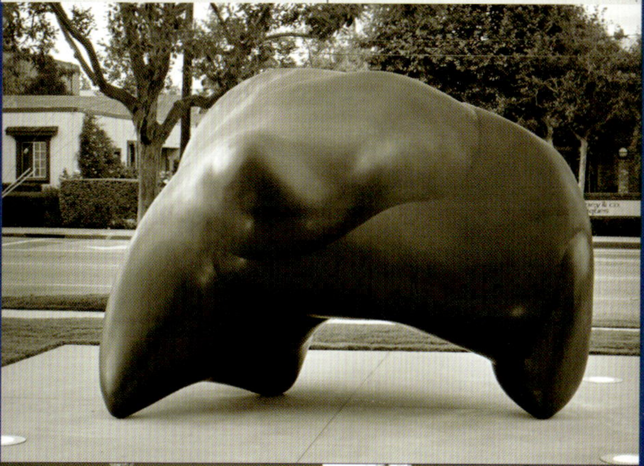

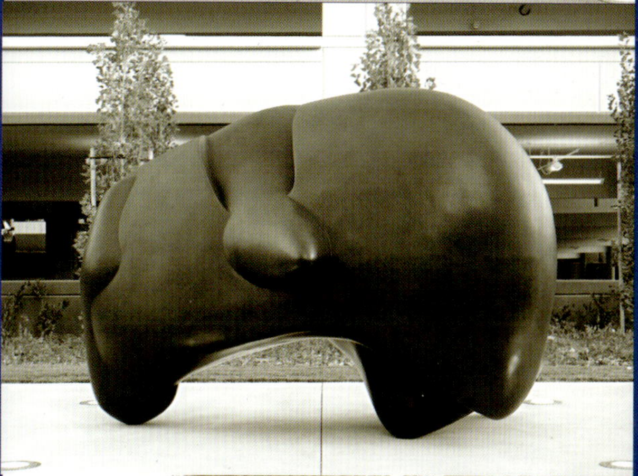

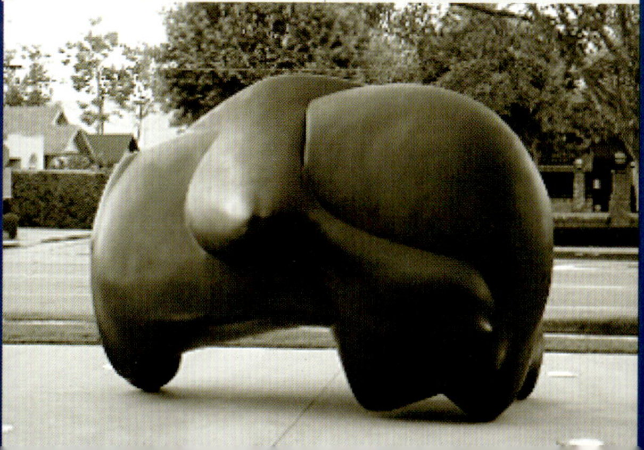

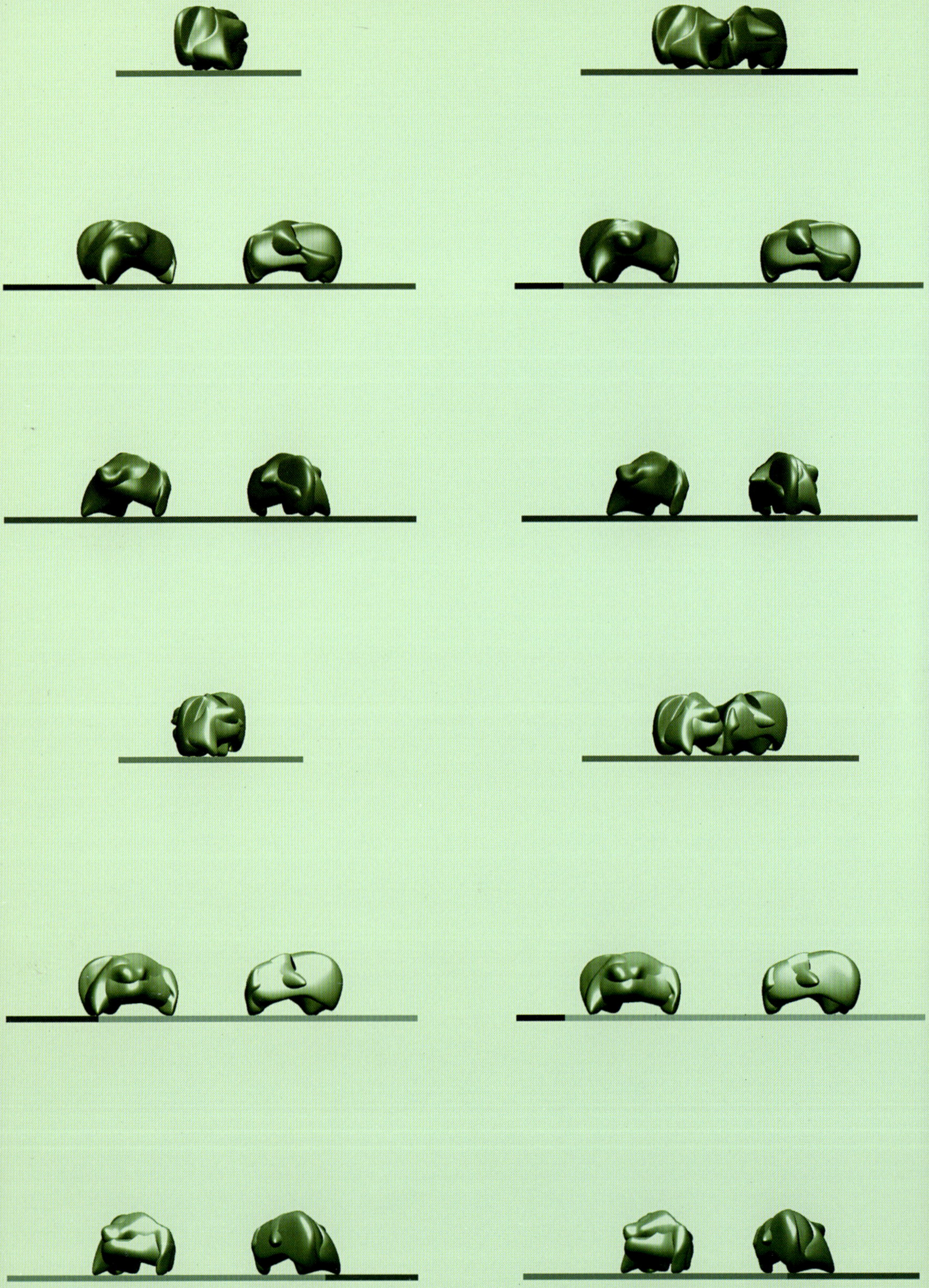